A Match Struck in Akron

GUS STEFANOW

Published by GUS STEFANOW, 2024.

While every precaution has been taken in the preparation of this book, the publisher assumes no responsibility for errors or omissions, or for damages resulting from the use of the information contained herein.

A MATCH STRUCK IN AKRON

First edition. September 1, 2024.

ISBN: 979-8224805716

Written by GUS STEFANOW.

Table of Contents

Where does a deep abiding love begin, thrive, and continue endlessly? How does one define what makes a relationship last through decades of turmoil, chaos, and pain? There are no easy answers or simple formulas that ensure success. Humans cannot follow a simple ten-step plan for marital success to "make it" as a couple. When Gusty Stefanow met Emily Brummett in a small diner in Akron, Ohio, in 1948, sparks flew. Each instantly felt that the person they saw was the one they'd want from that moment forward. This book is an attempt to honor the comical bliss my parents survived for fifty-five years. I dedicate this book to them with some irreverence and lots of love. Enjoy the madness!

CHAPTER ONE

A fifty-five-year romance needs a solid foundation to fully appreciate its longevity. Love, or the simplified version that sprouts when two sets of eyes connect for the first time, can be cultivated as time goes by, as we'll see in the case of my parents, Gusty and Emily Stefanow.

As Dad taught, *ladies first* is the way to proceed. Even before the onset of World War II, Mom's life became one of constant upheaval and struggle. She lived a nomadic lifestyle for years.

Mom's arrival on earth came with issues. Her mother, called "Mamaw," had a difficult pregnancy from start to finish. Mamaw's legal name was Jemima, but nobody with any sense dared call her that. Oddly enough, she went by Jay, Jaybird, or Bunt her whole life. (An Appalachian tradition, I surmised.) A tough Kentucky mountain woman, she feared little in life. Mom came along during the Great Depression as a blessing and another mouth to feed. Poverty became the only thing in abundance.

Mom developed a fever, and doctors were scarce as hen's teeth in the holler known as Frog Level near Huntin' Shirt, now known as Manchester, Kentucky. Mamaw's first husband, Johnny, rode off on horseback to get medicine and fetch the doctor. On his return trip, the young man got bucked from his horse and thrown into a nearby creek. He remounted the horse at the height of a cold winter without losing the medicine. He caught pneumonia and died on Mom's first birthday in 1932.

Mamaw stayed single for years, taking a job with the Works Progress Administration that required her to leave Mom with her maternal grandmother, also named Emily. This arrangement lasted about three years before Mamaw found a beau named Willie. Though eight years her junior, the situation worked for both. He worked in the coal mines and came with strong, handsome features. After tiring of the danger and the pay, he (known to us as Papaw) went into farming to earn a living. Physical, violent fireworks from stress and dueling personalities meant the "lovebirds" crowned each other with everything from fireplace pokers to ax handles. At least nobody got shot.

Papaw's chicken farm lasted for several years before the Depression got worse, and he got stuck with animals to feed on acreage that was unaffordable.

"Chicken in the mornin', chicken in the evenin', chicken at supper time" became the family refrain they grew disgusted with rapidly. (Mom never ate fish or fowl for the rest of her life.)

Mamaw worked to help support her little family. She got paid 25 cents a day to work the fields of those who were better off. With Mom a youngster, Mamaw chose to leave her at home. To ensure that Mom stayed in place, Mamaw removed a feather from her bed and placed it in the doorway of their cabin. To keep Mom restrained, Mamaw told her a monster would appear from the feather and eat her if she tried escaping. Psychological warfare indoctrination started early for Mom. Fear of everything was purposely pounded into her developing brain and psyche, creating wounds that festered later in life.

The family faith combined Christianity, mountain lore, and sheer superstition. For regular churchgoers, biblical literacy lacked a strong orthodoxy. Allowing "additions" to a Christian-based upbringing was typical and expected where Mom grew up. The environment promoted à la carte adherence to a belief system. Mix and match religion, if you will.

Spill salt on the table? A remedy meant throwing more over both shoulders and blessing the house. Anyone with an upturned broom in the corner of their house practiced witchcraft. If one forgot something on a trip from home, the vehicle turned around, and every blessed soul counted to thirteen, so everything went well with the journey. Bad omens came in threes. Crossing silverware on the dinner table meant death for an unsuspecting soul. One always had to leave through the same door one entered. If one's hand itches, expect to receive money or shake hands with a stranger. These samples were deeply embedded in Mom's childhood and nearly consumed her as an adult.

Mom experienced a few bright spots in her childhood. A dog to play with when Mamaw worked most of the day provided a blessing. Being able to visit a friend named Harlan Sanders became a treat. Mr. Sanders, a friendly old guy the family knew well before his fame in the 1960s, sat on his porch swing with Mom, telling tales about the old days. He hoped to one day keep a job that supported his family and led to the franchising of the world-famous "Kentucky Fried Chicken" empire.

Economics improved in the latter part of the '30s, and Papaw moved the family to Akron, Ohio, for work in rubber or defense plants. His brother Hoss secured a job and a place to stay. Mom thoroughly rejoiced to have such luxuries as running water and indoor plumbing! It didn't last, though, and a year later they went back to Kentucky. In Mom's view, this yo-yo effect kept the family going "backward." She only steeled herself to run away. She wandered off more with each passing year. She became the *Original Kentucky Wildcat* to the ones who knew her best!

Once in the Bluegrass State, Papaw returned to the mines for steady, dangerous work. Mamaw tilled the land, kept the cupboards as full as possible, and sometimes put Mom in school. Mom fell behind the other children and hated returning, especially since she treasured her stay in Ohio. Irregular attendance haunted Mom throughout her whole life, and she struggled to find any semblance of formal education. She learned "street smarts" and put them to use. Living by "hook or crook" became a reality.

After a couple more KY-OH-KY excursions, Mom was tired of the nomadic lifestyle. In her early teens, she openly rebelled against both parents on a daring, almost suicidal path.

"Mom, when we go back to Ohio, I am stayin' there! You got me used to them fancy toilets, runnin' water, and modern stuff so that you can have Kentucky!" Mom blurted out one day.

Mamaw bristled and would have none of the argument, no way, shape, or form.

"Little lady, you can think all you want about where we're livin', but you're gonna stay where you been a-planted until old enough to take off!"

"I'm tellin' you, I ain't livin' down here and a-marryin' some ol' boy in overalls with a chaw in his mouth! We get back to Ohio, and I swear I'll marry the first forner who asks me!"

Undeterred, Mamaw ended the conversation with a "We'll see about that. That'll be the day you marry some dad-gummed forner!"

Before long, Papaw was offered a construction job with a union company, which he readily accepted. The DeBartolo Corporation needed skilled carpenters in northeast Ohio, and there were jobs aplenty in the post-war building boom! Housing was tough, but with a brother already having a place, the family set sail again to greener pastures. Akron, Ohio, became the landing spot for peace and prosperity. The Buckeye State experienced tremendous growth, and Mom's family fit right in.

Dad's trek from northeast Pennsylvania to Akron came about after an upbringing in Hazelton that he became fortunate to have lived through. With immigrant parents speaking broken English from Greece and Poland, respectively, Dad's large family suffered from want. Pop Stefanow, an itinerant chef from Greece, came to the United States as a nine-year-old stowaway, as family legend tells it. Mom Stefanow went to the U.S. via Poland. With Pop taking jobs outside the local area to feed his family, Mom took care of seven children and scrubbed floors in the evenings to scratch out a tough living. In the Stefanow family, poverty breathed palpably.

Dad became the baby of the family via a family tragedy that haunted him his whole life. Uncle Leo, the youngest Stefanow child, drowned at a family picnic when Dad was very young. Dad couldn't comprehend the loss, but a nun explained it to him in a way he understood. She likened life's length to the light of a candle at birth. Candle sizes vary, but regardless of size, when each candle burns out, God brings that soul home. Although not easy, Dad grasped the idea as best he could. His zeal for life, spontaneity, and inability to control impulses may lie in his comprehension of Uncle Leo's accident.

Seeing the brevity of life, Dad relaxed family rules and acted up while his father was out of town. The list of "Little Rascal-like" adventures might fill a book on its own merits. Examples come from Dad's recollection of growing up. His appearance reminded many of a character called "Froggy," a boy with thick glasses and a voice that peeled paint from walls. Dad accepted ribbing from siblings but not classmates looking for trouble. He and his brothers fought routinely, training him to handle bullies.

One day, Dad got bored hanging around doing nothing and got friends together for fun. Evening came, so they went to the local lumber yard and broke out every window in the building. When the police sirens blared, where did they run? Of course, they confidently hid inside the local precinct where *nobody* would look for them! Model citizens.

As a teen, Dad and his pals liked to play a game of "smash-your-neighbor's face," and the gang loved it. The idea involved finding another teen of equal size, "sucker-punching" them in the face, and moving on rather rapidly.

Late one Saturday night, Dad scanned the streets and picked out a victim. Just a block over, one was minding their own business when they came into view. Dad crossed the street to welcome the soul into a new awareness.

Dad, smiling, stepped directly into the path of the unknown patsy. He drew back his fist and firmly planted it into the guy's skull! The guy fell backward as Dad's buddies rejoiced from a distance. Game on!

The "boy" sprang to his feet and, with the arms of an undersea octopus, pummeled Dad with a series of blows, punctuated by a judo chop to his midsection that left him gasping for air and eating sidewalk. Dad's friends arrived to help him; afraid their fate would be the same if they intervened.

This "boy" approached the light, and everyone saw the supposed teenager. The light revealed the man's stocky build and five o'clock shadow. The *man* kindly reached down to pull Dad to his feet, explaining that, as a United States Marine, he'd come home on leave to visit his girlfriend.

Dad's buddies left him and ran away as fast as their legs would take them. Dad quickly apologized, shook the man's hand, and stumbled home. He taught his kids this lesson: Don't start fights with anyone! He preached that the Stefanow family didn't start fights but did *finish* them.

Dad's family received entrepreneurial instincts at birth, especially when looking through the lens of history. His enterprising idea was to go to the local supper club (Genetti's), set up a paid-parking booth, and don an outfit from a second-hand store. He made money hand over fist for several weekends, thrilling the family with the "easy-money" exploits. His business crashed when a new Cadillac pulled into the lot one evening. When quizzed by the annoyed driver about paying to park and its authorization, Dad proudly proclaimed, "Why, Mister Genetti set this up!"

"What? Cried the incensed man, I am Mister Genetti!"

Thus, the business folded up that night as Dad left in a hurry, tossing his uniform and cap as he ran!

Dad routinely tested Mom Stefanow's patience when Pop worked out of town. He'd apologize, repent, and then repeat the sequence. Being the youngest meant getting a certain amount of grace not readily afforded to the other children. It ended in a surprise one late at night.

Did Dad have a bedtime with Pop out of town? Sure, Mom Stefanow routinely checked in on him because he'd prowl the streets after dark. When bored, he always returned home.

After hanging out at the railyards, busting streetlights, or rigging free pinball games, Dad strolled home like the original gangster wannabe. He enjoyed smoking as a teen because he'd secretly done it since age nine, but not quite so openly as this night.

He hopped over the locked gate, humming a contemporary tune, victorious in his defiance. What he could not see in the dark was the figure of Pop Stefanow sitting motionless on the porch swing.

Dad flipped his finished cigarette, stepped up to the door, and searched for his key. Judgement Day thrust itself upon him.

Pop gave no dissertation. He gave no words of wisdom or warning when he rose. He calmly looked into his son's eyes, pulled back a massive meat hook fist, and clobbered Dad into a flowerbed in the front yard.

As Dad awoke, Pop stood over him and kindly said, "You no more lie to your mother, you get me?"

Dad's jaw sat slightly out of square, but he muttered that he understood. He knew his father to be tough but fair. There was no need for a rematch!

Dad's wandering led him to a Navy recruiting office. Though only sixteen years old, he said he was eighteen. One call home, and Mom Stefanow set the record straight. Dad set his sights on the Merchant Marines, and Mom Stefanow agreed to sign him up for a non-combatant role in the Pacific. Weeks later, the Japanese surrendered, and most troops, even two of Dad's older brothers, began returning home.

Uncle Stan served in the Army during WWII and went on to have an excellent job in Akron, Ohio. He and Aunt Marge settled in and readied for the post-war prosperity the country envisioned.

Mom and Pop Stefanow still had their youngest at home to corral and give directions. After a few more run-ins with authority, Dad needed a change. With Uncle Stan just one state away, the family joined him in the Buckeye State.

The Pennsylvania-Kentucky collision course set itself for both clans. Americans would forever link nomadic lifestyles with very diverse backgrounds and experiences. People readied for a better life; if that meant moving to get it, so be it! If the post-war stars aligned, anyone not on board would miss their chances! Only time would tell if the world could handle it.

CHAPTER TWO

Pop Stefanow quickly got a job in Akron, given his culinary skills. Everyone settled into a routine, striving to adapt to the hustle and bustle of a growing American city. Jobs were plentiful for the average person who desired to lead a productive life. Things went well with Dad's move. Optimism ruled the day.

Over at Mom's place, Papaw's great union job with benefits meant he could retire in his later years. Mom and Mamaw clashed, with head-butting becoming the day's highlight for the mother-daughter duo. Mom wanted the more remarkable things in life that Mamaw saw as less critical. She and Papaw covered the basics of food, clothing, and shelter. Mom being ungrateful or just expecting more in the newfound post-war prosperity? Mom decided to earn her own money in the world. It went over like a turd in a punchbowl.

"Mom, I am gettin' a job, and *soon*! Mom declared.

"You're gonna do what, lady?" Mamaw replied.

"You heard me! Ain't nothing wrong with your ears! I am gettin' work to buy things I want!" Mom said, raising her voice for emphasis.

"Emily, you sass me *once* more like that, and I'll slap the lips off your face," Mamaw roared! No one doubted that she promised anything in the physical realm.

Mom toned down the conversation but insisted on having a job to pay for "extras" her parents saw as nonsense. Makeup, jewelry, and new dresses she'd splurge on with disposable income. Months of constant badgering allowed Mom to get her way. This pattern continued throughout her entire life. She embodied the tenacity of a fox in a hen-house! Her constancy of purpose surpassed that of anyone on God's green earth.

Mom's first job offer came after months of the standoff with Mamaw. Each waited for the other to blink. A friend told Mom of a jewelry counter downtown that needed someone for the cosmetics counter. Part-time work and bus line availability sealed the deal. After Mamaw and Papaw wrangled over the idea, Mom got her job!

Mom started at the jewelry counter in downtown Akron right on schedule. A beautiful, petite young lady, she sold cosmetics to the "luxury-starved" public. Years of rationing everything created pent-up demand. More women entered the workforce out of necessity during the war, and the income they earned proved quite handy. Mom wanted to spend money not so much on a career as on the independence that fueled her to keep earning something of her own.

While the money came steadily at the jewelry counter, Mom sought jobs more to her liking. When a server job opened at a local diner, it seemed like the answer and proved life-altering.

The diner offered comfort food to local factory workers, businesspeople, and anyone wanting a speedy meal at a fair price. Mom's "regulars" kept her on her toes until mere days before Christmas 1948, when a tall, dark, skinny stranger appeared. He showed no interest in the food and did not take his eyes off *her*.

The stranger didn't speak, but Mom felt his eyes on her with every move. His handsome, good looks caught her eye, but what if he were a maniac? Several days in a row, he ordered a coffee and then repeatedly played "Maybe You'll Be There" by Betty Jean Rhodes. Customers and staff were alike tired of the song *until* it played to the point of madness.

One of the cooks pulled Mom aside and told her he worried about her walk home. He wrapped up a small knife and put it in her hand. He told her to use it if necessary because nobody could walk her home. Mom's anxiety elevated when her shift ended, but she put the knife in her coat for safekeeping. The December cold made concealment very easy. She did *not* camouflage her fears, though.

The handsome stranger followed as she crossed the street for the short walk home. Across a busy intersection, she felt his presence and heard his footsteps. Two more crossings and she'd be home, but as he approached, Mom sprang into action. No, he was sneaking up on an Irish-English-Cherokee woman.

Whirling around with the blade visible, she startled the man! A sneer fell over her face as she tried to look fearless!

"Wait a minute, ma'am, I don't mean you no harm!' Dad yelled out when confronted.

"Mister, one more move and I will cut you seventy-two different ways!" Mom responded.

"Hey, I just wanted to walk home with you, that's it! Dad replied.

"Look, I saw you a-eyeballin' me for days in the diner like some kinda weirdo. No way you follow me home, mister! No way!" Mom insisted.

"Okay, but how about we talk on your next shift, okay, just talk! I'm going to be in there anyway. Nobody can stop me doin' that", Dad now insisted.

"Suit yourself, buddy, but I got people a-watchin' you every day!" Mom replied and hustled away down the street. For good measure, she did not go the direct route home, hoping to keep Dad in the dark about where she lived.

When she arrived home, she told her folks about the encounter. Both were happy that she confronted the strange man and more content that she'd carve him up if he made any unwelcome advances. The incident made her uneasy about returning, so she took a few days off to ease the tension.

On Mom's first day back at the diner, the crew told how her "stalker" popped in each day to get a look-see for her. His determination to speak with her and willingness to chance a police escort off the property only exacerbated the situation.

Sure enough, Dad showed up, ordered his cup of coffee, and stared away. Mom became unnerved, but something in the stranger's eyes mesmerized her. Well-dressed, as usual, the man even appeared sophisticated for one so young. Every other employee kept eyes on Dad as he sipped his coffee, then zipped over to the jukebox for that *same* song! Mom had to speak to him, or the staff might toss him out on his ear.

"Okay, buddy, what are you doing here again?" Mom asked.

"Hey, I just got off my shift at Crest Bakery and am in the neighborhood. I thought I'd stop by and hope you'd speak!" Dad answered.

"You got everyone, including my parents, thinkin' you're some weirdo by doing this every day. I guess I don't understand." Mom trailed off, and Dad jumped back in.

"No, I only wanted to talk! You are beautiful and just what I'm looking for! I can't stay away!"

Mom did not buy what Dad was trying to sell at this point. Curious and flattered by what the handsome man said with his eyes, he appeared as no country bumpkin with hayseeds in his clothes and dirt under his nails. He gave the impression that he'd be someone going places. Her unease dropped with each coffee refill. He even stopped playing the song he had tried to woo her with.

Mom's shift ended, yet she wanted no part of him following her home. He told her "Same time, same place" for the next day if she'd be working, and she agreed.

Mom's folks gave her the interrogation of her life when she got home. What, she talked to this strange, forward man! Papaw looked over his gun rack and told Mom to "pick one" IF she wanted this "boy" to stay away. Mamaw railed about her youth while Mom reminded her that one could be an old maid at sixteen "down home," so, nearing eighteen, the time had come. She lived in the Big City and meant to live that way. The discussion turned ugly, as many had in the past. Undeterred, Mom backed down from no threats. Mamaw mentioned her barrenness in her youth, and Papaw muttered under his breath, as was his typical pattern.

Dad sailed in on cloud nine when he got back home. Mom and Pop saw the glow of his happiness from the street below their apartment. Both stared at each other as Dad popped in the door. They knew it'd be a big day!

"That girl at the diner, well, she talked to me today! Yeah, no knives were pulled or anything! She is gorgeous, and that place has the best coffee!" Dad smirked.

Pop sat there, disgusted, thinking but saying nothing. Mom Stefanow appeared more interested and worried at the same time. She asked some questions. Her English improved, so Pop let her translate many times.

"Gusty, how do you know this girl is not some crazy person? Who threatens my boy with a knife on a walk home? No, she's crazy. You're crazy, too, if you go for her!"

Dad's folks had many more questions he did not want to answer.

"Is she Greek? Pop asked emphatically. Dad knew what that meant and answered too slowly for Pop's liking.

"Is she Greek? Pop said with more volume.

"No, she's not Greek, and I don't think she's Polish either, Mom!" Dad responded.

Now, Mom Stefanow did the sign of the cross, and Pop chattered on something in broken English about Dad's lack of brains.

Mom Stefanow, scared and curious, needed to know more about this young mystery woman.

"Where is she from? Her people, I mean? She not, uh, what you call, uh, hill-people, no hillbilly, right?"

Dad came up with something quick. He stammered because he knew from the accent that Mom had fallen off the turnip truck from someplace south. Dad found the fight inside him lit, even if it meant defying the immigrant parents who wanted the best for him.

Mom's next shift at the diner put a little more spring in her step. She saw a different side of the stranger, a sincerity that held her attention. Dad came in, and Mom's face lit up. Her concerned co-workers eyed each other with disbelief. The diner became a match-making attraction right in front of them!

The next day, December 1948, the same scenario played out. Dad got off his bakery shift and appeared at his "second home," as his parents began to call it. Mom poured another cup of coffee, and the two youngsters followed up with the conversation. Things took a serious tone this day.

"What, uh, what would you do if I asked you to marry me, Emily?" Dad boldly blurted out.

"Well, why would I marry you, Gusty?" Mom said almost too quickly for anyone to eavesdrop again.

"Alright then, we'll get married!" Dad boasted!

Neither potential adult confidently revealed what took place to their respective families. Did any of that stop them from marrying? No, it didn't.

They both agreed that each needed to meet the other's parents right away. Dad suggested that he meet Mom on the night walk home if Mom decided. Comfortable with him now, she went along with the idea.

Mom's shift ended, and she cleaned up and grabbed her purse as she exited. On the walk, she tried to describe her mother, but Dad didn't care about it either way. Naturally, neither exposed their actual plans. Long courtship went out of style in their minds. They found their one person and planned to get married very soon. Strategies need proper planning.

Things went very well as they plotted and they walked. Once up to Mom's porch, Mamaw stood outside in the twilight of the day, waiting. She didn't like being taken by surprise.

They went up the walkway to the door as Mamaw stepped out of the shadows. Dad's shock manifested right away!

"Holy Christopher, it's the devil!" Dad exclaimed, running backward to the sidewalk, taking off in a streak that could be compared to lightning on a stormy summer night.

Enraged, hurt, and speechless, Mom looked to Mamaw as she stood there with coffee wires in her hair, making it appear to stand on end. She must have looked like a hillbilly Medusa in her nighttime ensemble.

"Well, Emily, that'll be the end of that boy, won't it? I don't know what he saw, but it scared him to death!" Mamaw babbled, scowling and going inside. Papaw got the rundown and laughed as he did. The end of a boy? The problem with Mom's independence worked itself out well!

Mom didn't believe her bad luck. How rude! Anyone can be startled, but Mom couldn't forgive rudeness at the crucial first meeting!

True to form, Dad returned to the diner the next day. He confidently carried in sets of rings. Mom hesitated to approach his seat, bring coffee, and try to smile. She didn't hide the hurt over the incident from the night before.

"Emily, said Dad, I am sorry for running last night. I got scared! I ain't seen nothin' like that!"

Mom looked at him skeptically, but his charm came out. He began working emotionally *overtime* to smooth out the debacle. This intro would happen over and over again for the next five decades.

Mom loved the shiny new rings, but didn't accept them before Dad met her parents. Mom hatched a plan for Dad to meet Papaw and Mom's Aunt Odie to get the ball rolling. How could he know that Mamaw, hair fixed and wearing a lovely dress, *pretended* to be the aunt left behind in Kentucky? With these families, the surprises have no end.

Dad escorted Mom after her diner shift the next day, eager to make amends with Papaw and the aunt. The man headed directly into a buzz saw. A chainmail suit might have come in handy.

In what became an impromptu engagement party, Dad needed to impress. Mom introduced Papaw, who loved Dad from the first handshake, and her "Aunt Odie." Papaw looked at Dad and said, "Good luck, buddy, good luck!"

Dad spoke with Mom's "Aunt" for almost two hours before he asked when Mamaw would arrive. To his shock, Mom revealed that the well-dressed, affable lady he'd conversed with was the specter he'd seen! (No chain mail required!) Feeling stupid, Dad apologized profusely for running away. Indeed, Mamaw was no devil, at least on the outside. That debate raged on for decades afterward.

The next stop in Mom's trial-by-fire came with Mom and Pop Stefanow. Dad warned her that Pop's cantankerous nature and poor English were troublesome. He told her to nod and pretend to understand since this custom of others usually worked well.

Mom Stefanow embraced Mom from the very onset of the relationship. Praised for her looks and demeanor, she'd be good enough for the Stefanow family, despite her hillbilly roots!

Pop's standoffishness made Mom uneasy at first. Mom met him and felt a chill in the room. He called her something in his Greek-English lingo that she felt couldn't be a compliment, but she nodded and smiled, per Dad's instruction. Dad knew Pop would come around and love his future daughter-in-law, regardless of her roots.

Both Mom and Dad were considered minors in 1948. Ohio law required men to be 21 to marry, while females aged 16 to 18 needed their father's consent. Papaw did not go for Mom marrying anyone at seventeen, but Mamaw looked at it differently. It took sneaky family intervention to make the blessed union a reality. Kentucky to the rescue?

CHAPTER THREE

Neither set of parents foresaw what was happening right in front of them. Sure, the two kids *liked* each other quite a bit, but marriage seemed premature for them. Just telling their parents they want to get married would get fierce resistance. At this point, Mom and Dad felt engaged, at least in their minds. Nobody took that seriously except the two with sparkles in their eyes.

Mom's ally, Uncle Shafter, Aunt Odie's husband, proved nobody's favorite. His streak of defiance and the "Goodtime Charlie" persona left indelible marks on Mom's personality. Mom became the hellion, no doubt, and it went with everything she wore. Uncle Shafter loved the grit in his niece. He minded not one bit being the resident troublemaker.

Ohio's laws were nothing trifling, but Kentucky showed no restrictions to interfere with one's marital bliss. Uncle Shafter hatched a plan to take the young couple south to marry legally in an elaborate deception. Stealth planning went into motion.

Dad's infatuation with Mom led him to go to great lengths to marry her. He lied to Mom and Pop about heading to Cleveland to join the Army, saying he'd be back in a year or two, thereby giving them sufficient time to get from Akron to London, Kentucky, for the wedding.

Uncle Shafter picked up Mom, who felt she was running away despite having a letter from her folks allowing the marriage. She welcomed the change, whatever her new life brought.

The long drive included Uncle Shafter's stories and Dad's voracious appetite. Tall and skinny, Dad consumed more than men, much heavier. At a roadside diner, Mom excused herself as Dad ate two of the daily specials. Uncle Shafter marveled at the exhibition and stayed while Dad ate as if it were his last meal.

Once Dad ordered three meals, Uncle Shafter retreated to the car, too. He had never seen a human being consume what Dad had. He joked with Mom that she should consider buying a grocery store because she would *need* one!

At the Courthouse in London, Kentucky, the "real" Aunt Odie met the gang to witness the blessed union. Dad wore his best suit, and Mom got a thrift-store wedding dress to set fifty-five years of love and combat in motion. The adventure began.

Where do newlyweds celebrate their honeymoon when they're cash-strapped? In January 1949, one might guess Lexington, Louisville, or Cincinnati. Mom and Dad went to Pa Smith's place after the ceremony, with rollaway beds instead of the honeymoon suite. The uncles and aunts shared the space, so both newlyweds missed out on one simmering part of marriage.

A large country breakfast arrived early the following day. Aunt Odie prepared the bacon, eggs, biscuits, and bacon gravy for everyone. Dad, never shy about eating, emptied an entire platter of eggs onto his plate. He took half the bacon, drawing the watchful eyes of every hungry person there. Mom elbowed him (A precedent throughout Dad's life.) with a rib shot, saying nobody came between a hungry hillbilly and breakfast!

Pa Smith, the ranking patriarch, looked astonished but spoke up. No hungry buzzard surpassed Dad's appetite!

"Ode...ODIE, get some more breakfast for everyone! And Big Em, you let that feller eat like he's used to!"

Aunt Odie almost jumped out of her skinny self when she sprang from the table to order more food. Her disgusted glance at Dad went unnoticed, and she returned to work upon command, cussing under her breath.

Once the shock wore off over what the clan witnessed, small talk ensued around the table. Dad struggled to understand the jargon and accents. He knew he didn't fit in, but made cracks that endeared him to everyone.

"Folks, you gotta know I bought Emily her first pair of shoes! Yeah, I stuffed rocks into the toes to make her feel comfortable," Dad barked.

Everybody knew better but chuckled along, hoping this "forner" would fit in... someday.

Mom did not sit still and ignore the first marital salvo in one of the longest-running "wars" in holy matrimony. She nodded her head, prepping a good comeback.

"Well, if you all think that's somethin', wait 'til you hear what my ol' forner asked me last night. He needed a bathroom, and I told him the outhouse sat out front, way past the cornfield. He stumbled out of here, took care of business, and came back a-shakin' his head. Know what he asked me?" "Emily, I used that toilet, but I'll be darned. There was no handle to flush it!"

Everyone howled as Dad shook his head, saying he never said that! He tried to backpedal, but the laughter drowned out anything he said to refute Mom's story!

The day went on with visits, and everyone welcomed the newlywed duo. For dinner, Mom decided to visit more kinfolk at her Aunt Nan's place. None of Mom's relatives would be considered well-off, but they shared with others. Aunt Nan became known near and far as one of Kentucky's best cooks, but Dad put that claim to the test.

Aunt Nan's farmhouse bustled with activity in preparation for the newlywed's arrival. Word had yet to get around about Dad's appetite, but to be sure, plenty of food awaited.

Cheers arose when the happy twosome knocked on the front door. After the hugs and kisses, the well-wishers lined up to eat buffet-style. Mom and Dad hung around the back, trying to be polite. Mom warned Dad to take the food given and leave something for others this time.

When Dad arrived, he found no plates available, not even a saucer. Aunt Nan got embarrassed but found Dad a half-plate from an old cupboard. She apologized, but Dad proved his graciousness.

As the meal wound down and the conversation waned, Aunt Nan wanted a full report on the fried chicken and ham she'd cooked. She'd noticed how often Dad returned to the buffet with that cracked half-plate. He'd eaten an entire chicken by himself.

"Gusty, how'd you like this here meal we fixed for you?" Aunt Nan asked.

Not sure how much he'd eaten, Dad decided to have fun with people he did not know.

"Well, Aunt Nan, I tell you. That food's so good that I even put down half the plate!"

Aunt Nan never cracked a smile, sitting with a look of disdain on her face, while others laughed nervously. Mom became mortified at being seated by her man. Dad looked around for allies and found none.

Everyone got up from the table to retire elsewhere. Aunt Nan grunted something under her breath and left the house for the fields outside. Mom got Dad by the arm and insisted they leave. Aunt Nan did not speak to Dad for the next three years.

The young couple's eventual return to Ohio and the complications with Dad's folks marked tense times. Mamaw and Papaw owned rental properties and rented out half of their duplex to the married kids for five dollars per week.

Mom and Pop Stefanow were somewhat ignorant of the plan to marry. They supported the engagement but wanted a longer courtship. They also wanted a Catholic ceremony that Mamaw and Papaw did not. Disinformation cropped up from somewhere that said Mom's sins needed sweeping from the church by the priest in a symbolic gesture because of her Baptist/Pentecostal upbringing. Mom would not convert amid the suspicions and accusations. The "easy" way to marry meant eloping. Both agreed that Christian beliefs were not to be one-sided. Any children from the union would have to see Catholic-Protestant views and one day decide for themselves which to follow.

Once Dad introduced Mom as his wife to his parents, three things emerged. One meant that Mom Stefanow accepted Mom as "her hillbilly self" from the beginning. The second suggested that Pop Stefanow continued to call Mom an unintelligible name, making it difficult to know his true feelings. A stern man with an angry streak, he proved a rascal because he *wanted* to be. The third and most hurtful event came when Dad realized Pop Stefanow refused to speak to him. A cardinal rule in the Stefanow clan meant no tolerance for lying. Lying to Pop about his whereabouts and the wedding couldn't be overlooked. No atonement existed for the offense. Pop Stefanow did not speak directly to his son for years afterward. Mom Stefanow called her husband a "stubborn Greek" who also adhered to standards he expected everyone to follow.

A few weeks into sharing the duplex with the in-laws, the fireworks began. At home from a rough day at the bakery, Dad came into an empty house, yet again, and he wouldn't have any part of it.

Without the benefit of the after-work shower, Dad stormed over to his in-laws to find Mom there gabbing with Mamaw. His fiery brown eyes and his father's Greek temper spilled out in the living room. His wife would be home each day to greet him! She'd be there to welcome him after a grueling shift. He presented where he stood.

Mom's defiance and "easily-insulted" personality struck back as forcefully as given. She relished no idea of dancing to any tune like a one-trick pony! Mamaw, for her part, rushed them out the door to argue in their place before Papaw got home.

Their first of a lifetime's worth of disagreement went on for hours. It's fair to say that any items in the home became projectiles of punishment from mom's "live" right arm! Hit first, ask questions second became her mantra throughout her life, but both came to an accord. They had to move to another apartment a few blocks away for privacy. The landlords understood and agreed. Rent went up, but it proved worth it.

These were happy days for the loving couple. Dad volunteered to cook for a couple of reasons. Pop Stefanow trained Dad to prepare anything for even the pickiest palate. Dad loved the kitchen where he'd sing songs like "Catch a falling star and put it in your pocket, save it for a rainy day!" Mom fried *everything*, just as she'd learned. Shared kitchen duties led to skirmishes that neither side claimed victory in, but they worked themselves out. The truth is, the two lovebirds enjoyed each other's company.

Weeks into living away from the in-laws, they revealed another early crisis. Mom's grandfather passed away in Kentucky, and going "down home" was the only solution. Not having a car put them in a bind, so they paid a friend to take them. Dad made arrangements to leave work for a few days, and off they went.

Two days into the funeral arrangements, the friend-turned-livery agent left for Ohio without warning. The man couldn't miss work, so he left Mom and Dad no way home. Lesson learned.

By the time the couple returned to Akron, Dad had lost his job. The company showed no sympathy and said they'd replace him with five new people within 24 hours. What a blow in a very tough week.

New prideful couples want no help from family when times get tough. Dad lived the self-made man myth to the best of his ability.

Time without a paycheck and no savings account meant drastic measures came onto the horizon. Across the street from their apartment stood a city grocery store filled with necessities. Dad told Mom he'd steal if necessary to support them. Mom, calling him "dumber than a box of hammers," said he'd go to jail! Then what would happen?

Dad, always thinking, acted boldly. Maybe it was genetic or a personality trait he'd inherited. Literally hat in hand, Dad crossed the busy street and went inside the crowded market. He scanned the store for the manager and began his sob story.

"Mister, if you're hungry, out of work, and with no money, would you steal from your neighbor or ask for credit to pay back later?"

The manager seemed stunned by Dad's sincerity, and the brutal honesty took him off guard.

"Hey now, you get credit in here for your needs, my friend! Let me help you bag up anything you get! We call it credit, but someday, if you cannot pay it back, then count it as a gift," the manager insisted.

"No, I won't take advantage of you. You've got a business to run. You got overhead and bills to pay, too. I will take a few things, and when I get a job, I'll pay back your kindness." Dad replied.

In the interim, Mom Stefanow came to the rescue about Dad's job. She marched into Dad's boss's office to plead for her son's job. She asked what kind of monster fires a man attending a funeral. Her son, a good man, took his wife to a funeral, not a vacation.

The boss hesitated but relented because Mom Stefanow had no intention of leaving his office until he changed his mind. Dad took the call and did an impromptu jig! He repaid every cent to the grocer from his first paycheck back to work. The incident meant a victory for everyone.

Cars have always been budget-busters since the horseless carriages appeared in the early 1900s. Mass production made it easier for everyday Americans to afford it. When others discarded cars and the idea of planned obsolescence caught hold, the market for used automobiles took off. With the funeral debacle, Mom and Dad needed to find wheels. And find wheels they did.

Without asking for aid from their older, wiser parents, Mom and Dad went from used-car lot to lot like gypsies. Everything seemed too expensive for two kids on a very tight budget. Late one evening, just before closing time, a salesman slickered them in like lambs to slaughter, Detroit-style.

They went downstairs to a dimly lit garage/car preparation area. A used 1937 Chevrolet seemed just what they needed to get out on the open road! Per the salesman's pitch, the sixteen-hour drives down US-42 in Ohio and US-25 in Kentucky would get routine in this baby. Why, who else had this deal of a lifetime?

Suckered in and signing papers neither of them understood, they became proud owners of a piece of Americana! They bought a "classic" when nobody knew what they were. (In contemporary slang, we'd refer to it as a POS.)

The happy couple went to the dealership the next day to get the car. It was not in the showroom or the basement garage. Instead, the salesman parked it in the furthest spot from the building. Dad grabbed the keys and trotted out to get his treasure.

Dad's joy turned to shock when he caught the car in the sunlight. Rustier than a sunken ocean vessel (only missing barnacles!), the dents and dings in the body made one assume it had been in a demolition derby. The interior looked like John Dillinger had a shootout *inside it*! Dad's disgust turned to anger as he fired up his "prize" to grab Mom from the dealership!

Dad popped out of the car with the swagger he'd become known for, his face red as a stop sign. Mom shuffled out the door, Dad telling her to wait in the car. This action meant war!

Dad's shouting startled other customers and staff. The manager approached and suggested a side-room meeting, but robbing Dad put the dealership on shaky ground.

Dad's colorful language punctuated his feelings. He wanted restitution for the trickery. His argument went nowhere because he signed the papers and lost with no "right-of-refusal" three-day money-back laws on the books! He and Mom got stuck with twelve long months of payments on a car that belonged in the scrap heap. Growing up brought hard lessons along the way.

CHAPTER FOUR

Mom looked over a calendar and sighed. She called Mamaw to discuss the morning sickness and her heightened intolerance to certain odors, including garlic. In an odd twist, garlic bread became what Dad mostly baked at work. Everyone had to adapt somehow.

Dad, like many males, had no clue that Mom carried his child. The garlic wasn't his favorite, but he had a job. After standing near a 130-degree oven, he was required to shower when he got home. No problem. Being at work on the first shift meant he'd missed the morning issues most days. Mom wasn't sure about another mouth to feed. Deep down, Mom questioned if she'd be a better mother than her own. Critics would argue the point even today, but at least she would *try* to be different. Never known for subtlety, Mom broke the news her way.

Mom never "beat around the bush," as she called it, when delivering good or bad news. She accidentally blurted it out one day. Dad got up, shouted, danced a little jig, and told the grandparents. The happiest man most people knew had become even *more* joyful.

"Holy Christopher, Emily, we're havin' a baby! Wow! I can't wait to see the look on my parents' faces! Pop will ramble on about something in Greek, and Mom will praise Jesus for more grandkids! Man, what a day!" Dad yelled out as he danced in his most celebratory style.

Both sets of parents rejoiced, as can those expecting a grandchild! The hugs, kisses, and well-wishes came from both sides, although they showed the strain parenthood places on a young couple. Each family pledged to help in any way necessary, too. Another Stefanow would soon be running full speed!

A telephone call alerted the clan in Kentucky that Mom expected a child. While a call might have been good enough for most people, Mom wanted to see her kin's reactions in person. Dad, wary about the sixteen-hour trek on two-lane highways, reminded Mom about the state of their transportation.

"Emily, this car has bald tires, a bad radiator, and terrible headlights. You sure you want to go down home in this thing? We might make it there, but not back! Your people always want us to go south, but you know what I say? People in Hell want ice water! What if we get stuck in one of those hollers with no money to fix this heap! I ain't made of money!" Dad cautioned.

Mom couldn't be stopped, even if Jesus himself tried to change her mind. Mom's "constancy of purpose" and plain 'ol hillbilly stubbornness became hallmarks many said she'd inherited. Mamaw and Papaw never remembered Mom's first words, but she came from the womb arguing! The relatives down home had to know of the blessed event.

Dad worked his eight-hour bakery shift and then packed the old family hauler. Neither set of parents wanted to go and advised against it. Both families worried about their kids' safety in the heater. It fell on deaf ears.

US-42 in Ohio passed through quaint towns and villages, becoming busier in Columbus and Cincinnati. With most of the daylight gone, Dad piloted the old car into Kentucky on US-25 for the remainder of the journey. He and Mom looked like the Joads escaping Oklahoma. The wrath of the old Chevrolet began in earnest.

Whereas the "old road" in Ohio went through some form of civilization, US-25 in Kentucky appeared to follow grazing trails or "hollers" to locals, which suggested a drunken Billy goat was responsible. The road proved treacherous in the daylight hours, and the youngsters were in for the ride of their lives. Youthful optimism or two star-struck youths determined to defy logic spurred them on.

As the miles rolled along, Dad serenaded his young bride. Although he was no Frank Sinatra, his pipes proved good enough for the long ride.

"I don't want her, you can have her,
She's too fat for me, I don't want her,
You can have her, she's too fat for me, hey!"
Dad shouted in the song.

Mom's hackles went up over the silly song. Dad came close to a black eye from his pregnant wife.

"Oh, Emily, it's just the 'Too-fat polka!" I got more of them, like 'in heaven there is no beer, that's why we drink it here!' Polkas, you know, they're the songs of my people, and you're going to learn to dance them, or I'm not a Stefanow! You'll learn the steps, and you'll love it!" Dad spouted out.

"Jesus, Gusty, find somethin' a little better than these songs? Man, and you talk about hillbilly's crazy music!" Mom responded. (Mom learned the polka and danced it for fifty years.)

Dad thought for a while and produced some of the craziest things Mom had ever heard!

"Fishy, fishy in the brook,
Papa catch 'em on a hook,
Mama fry 'em in a pan,
Baby eat 'em like a man!"

With a disgusted look, Mom shook her head and begged Dad to stop. It seemed like some odd Doctor Seuss takeoff and was much less appreciated. Dad pressed on!

"Old man Kelly had a pimple on his belly,
His wife cut it off and made a jar of jelly!"

The origin of Mom's sensitive stomach may lie in this drive. She turned green, and Dad pulled over so she could "heave," as she called it. Mom's original "Eck, eck, eck, eck" sound needed to be patented! When it came to retching, Mom had no equal.

Dad's laughter dwindled as he realized Mom didn't care for his humor. Having three older brothers, Dad knew nothing sacred for a laugh. He crossed the line this time, but would do it plenty in the future.

The old Chevy needed water when Dad pulled in for gas. With the radiator full, Dad felt good at each stop. As the old car wound into the hills of Kentucky, Dad noticed the headlights getting dimmer and dimmer. Just in case, he'd gotten a couple of flashlights and fresh batteries from Papaw before they took off. No luxury in this travel existed whatsoever.

A short while later, Dad pulled over to check the lights with the car running. Sure enough, both worked with little functionality. With ingenuity, wire, and patience, the flashlights got fastened to the front fenders. Somehow, it worked, but for how long, nobody knew. The youngsters learned how to adapt and overcome.

Dad's youth and strength were admirable, but the day's weight made him tired. He refused to pull over for several reasons. There'd be no safe place to do it after dark; even though Mom suggested stopping, Dad would pull over *if* he felt like it. The miles rolled on, and Dad's heavy eyelids won out. Before he knew it, he slept comfortably at the wheel.

How long he'd been out cold is speculation. The twists and turns of the old road made it impossible to travel far without a collision. Mom slept a while, but it would not be for long. Guardian angels worked overtime on the jaunt south.

A bump here, a glide there, and long metal-on-metal scraping noises jostled Dad from his slumber! The old Chevy went left of the center line only to meet another oncoming night owl. Mom stayed motionless as the scene played out.

Dad screamed when both eyes opened! The damage came when he turned the steering wheel to the right. The old green beater he drove put a beautiful streak down the side of the new yellow Lincoln! Dad got his car over and onto the side of the road as Mom's eyes popped open, wondering why they had stopped. Not awake, Mom was startled by the action.

"A dog came out, Emily, I swear, and I swerved to miss it, and when I did, I sideswiped this other car!" said Dad, speaking fast when he lied, as some do.

"Well, you'd better go check that guy out! I hope everybody's okay! Lordy, Gus, you could have killed us! Stupid...stupid man!" Mom responded.

Dad got himself together and stumbled out of the car. The other driver surveyed the damage done to the less-than-pristine ride.

"Buddy, are you okay?" Dad asked.

"Yes, the man replied, but are you okay? I couldn't get out of your way no matter which side of the road I chose! What's wrong with you, pal? You have been drinkin'?"

Dad took offense over the inference and replied that he'd never drink and drive. The man walked over, looked at Dad's jalopy, shook his head, and started to speak, but Dad interrupted him.

"Hey, pal, I have insurance to fix your car, okay? I'll make it right!"

The man declined the offer and said he was a physician making a late-night house call. He asked Dad to pull over somewhere for the night and thanked him for his concern, but he declined Dad's offer. He would get his car fixed. He did not feel Dad's car showed any repair that would matter. To him, the vehicle appeared too far gone and well past its prime!

Dad shook the man's hand, hopped into his car, and sped away. He and Mom were awake for the remainder of the ride. He snickered as he relayed the conversation to Mom.

"Emily, so help me, that man felt sorry for us! He ain't hurtin' for money! He saw two broke kids in a heap, and showed mercy, I think! That's what you call good luck. Wow, I think we got very lucky! 'a tisket, a tasket, a brown and yellow basket....' As Dad broke out in song again.

Happy that no one got hurt, Mom worried about the fender flashlights. An all-night diner came up, and they bought more batteries, used the facilities, refueled, and prayed for daylight. On they went with newlywed love and faith to keep them focused.

The bright sun came up hours later at the first stop, Uncle Dick's tobacco farm.

The crop bringing the most dollars per acre meant leaving tobacco as king. Nobody ate it, but it paid far greater dividends for the hard work. Every kid did their part to run the communal business. Everyone carried their load if they wanted to eat—simple living on display.

The simple farmhouse across the hill from the enormous red barn in the cattle field set the scene for the picturesque farm. Modern conveniences like electricity and running water were still waiting. A double-hole outhouse proved as up-to-date as it got at the farm. Their way of life couldn't be for everyone, but it worked well for them. A nearby hog farm messed with Dad's sinuses.

"I smell something awful, Emily! Whew, it stinks down here on Tobacco Road! I hope it doesn't stink like this at Uncle Dicks!" Dad remarked.

Mom could not let that comment pass and began her famous retort.

"Gus, why, it's just your breath backfiring in your face! That's it! Whatever you do, don't insult my people with remarks like that! I want them to like you, go it? Your smart cracks ain't going to be appreciated here!" Mom responded.

Mom and Dad met with the usual ceremonial hugs from the entire clan. Somebody wallpapered the old farmhouse's unpainted interior walls and the entire living area with newspaper. Astonished at the ingenuity, he prepared a comment. He put his foot into his mouth each chance he got.

"You guys have done a lot with this place! I am going to love coming here. Why, you can read the sports page from five years ago or see the weather forecast from 1945! Miss an obituary? You got it on that far wall! Want to know how cheap groceries used to be at E.C. Porter's store? It's right here in black and white! History is right on your walls! Who decided which pages to use?" Dad asked in his usual sarcastic tone.

Mom glared at Dad with eyes of fire and insisted on words exchanged later. Everyone took note and nodded, saying nothing. Aunt Nan, as reported, had no intention of speaking to this "forner" ever again after the plate debacle, and she proved no fan of Dad's. The family did not welcome outbursts of mockery. Uncle Dick readied the youngsters for a glance around the farm, his pride and joy.

The high, sloping property on either side of the dirt road sectioned itself off with barbed wire. While not an ideal landscape, the relatives worked with what they had because no alternative existed. Survival mode became their daily operations tempo.

Mom and Dad both dressed snappily for a farm tour. Dad stepped into a pile of the unmentionable and was ready to *go*- no farm livin' for him. He'd been no fan of the outdoors, and everyone knew it. Part of meeting Mom's clan meant enduring things Dad didn't find comforting. His interest in animals lay only in how they fit on his plate. While Dad admired the simple contentment, the lifestyle held no grip on him.

The kids moved on to meet the rest of the clan and Mom's glory. Mom reminded Dad of the sarcastic cracks that he needed to correct. Dad, undeterred, would not comment on the décor they'd see. Besides, somebody needed to replace his dull headlights, and he wouldn't tick that person off. People got used to Dad's humor once they got to know him. Mom reminded him that for her clan to accept him, he had to *live* first! Despite his inability to stay serious for too long, Dad understood the challenge and put on his best act.

Once the visit reached total capacity, the headlights replaced, and well-wishing subsided, the two lovebirds headed back to Ohio, minus the silly songs that made Mom ill. Dad grabbed two sets of fresh batteries for the flashlights in case something went wrong in the jalopy again. They arose in the morning to take advantage of the daylight hours available for the grinding ride home.

The only eventful thing on the drive home became Dad's penchant for having a lead foot. He always bragged about "making good time" on any trip he drove. With Mom napping, he took advantage of the quiet and sped towards home. Dad saw speed limits like "Manufacturers Suggested Retail Price- MSRP" that nobody pays; therefore, no one gave credence.

As Dad zipped through Ohio, the flashing lights of the Ohio State Patrol appeared in his cracked rearview mirror. Doom!

Mom awoke to the sirens and sat up in her seat.

"Gus, what do they want? You...you speedin' in this ol' heap? And here I am resting so well. Lord, have mercy!" Mom lamented.

"Oh, Emily, I tried getting you home faster off this road! You know, in your condition...." Dad replied.

An official rest area came into view, and Dad got a brilliant idea, or so he thought. He borrowed a plan from Uncle Stanley's playbook for police stops.

"I'm pullin' in right here, and I'm runnin' into a stall. When the cop asks, tell them I got diarrhea, okay?" Dad said.

"Huh? Are you out of your dern mind? I ain't a-settin here and tellin' no cop you got the diarrhea, stupid man! I'll outrun you to the ladies' room, is what I'll do!" Mom responded.

Sure enough, two youngsters with no money for speeding tickets did as they said they would. Hand in hand, they raced to their respective stalls as the State Trooper pulled in behind them. Fifteen or twenty minutes later, both juveniles emerged to find the cop gone!

"Hahaha, Emily, my brother's trick worked like a charm! See, we wasted a little time, but the cop left just like that!" Dad said, snapping his fingers for emphasis.

"You say what you will, Gusty, but who's to know where he's a-hidin' up the road to get you! No, I ain't about to go back to sleep until we get home! You better not be a-speedin' with your child and me in this here car!" Mom warned.

Back home in Akron, Dad was tired of the bakery grind. The tiny shop had limited opportunities. Word on the street said jobs fell from the skies just thirty-five miles north in Cleveland like manna from Heaven. The lure gripped Dad, meaning he went on the hunt. The North Coast, the land of plenty, called his name, and he answered. The "good life" target lay just up the road.

CHAPTER FIVE

While commuting from Akron to Cleveland wasn't bad, it proved challenging for Mom, who was quite pregnant. Did she stick with the Akron doctors or switch if/when the move north came about? My folks had to look at all angles.

Friends steered Dad onto the streets of downtown Cleveland for work, and, as reported, every company took on help. Dad worked at one place and left the next day for a 10-cent-per-hour raise. If a boss looked crossways at him or suggested something he didn't want to do, he went to the next job, even if it was just across the street. By the time the calendar year ended in 1949, Dad had worked at twenty-six places of employment! Yes, twenty-six. His tax accountant jumped for joy in January.

As good fortune smiled on the employment horizon, Cousin Ralph contacted Mom and Dad about his apartment in Cleveland. He'd left Kentucky and gotten a construction job. He and his spouse were willing to split the rent, cooking, and cleaning chores if Mom and Dad were interested. In no time, the youngsters were moving to Cleveland- the Forest City!

Both parents displayed reservations about sharing living space with anyone, especially family. What would happen when the baby came? There were too many unanswered questions. Like any good son-in-law, Dad moved away from in-laws for less interference.

While the move to Cleveland proved uneventful, the parents were not thrilled with having to travel to see the new little one on the way. Mom immediately found a doctor who made her feel comfortable, and things fell into place.

Each night, the adults took turns cooking since eating out was beyond either couple's budget. Dad's familiarity with the kitchen came into question shortly after moving in.

Dad promised the gang mashed potatoes and meatloaf, a staple growing up. In a scene right out of a slapstick comedy, Dad salted his potatoes repeatedly but got no satisfaction. Does salt ever lose saltiness, he wondered? Dad rummaged through the cabinets, finding simple table salt and wondering what he'd been using. He turned the box around and saw the words "Epsom salts." his face turned pale, yet he told no one of his sins. Not even, as it turned out, his pregnant young bride.

Ralph displayed a powerlifter physique and ate like one. His voracious appetite proved legendary family-wide. His thin wife Evelyn could have worn a straw as a turtleneck sweater. Everyone gobbled up their food with enthusiasm as Dad picked at his meatloaf. The gastronomical disturbances commenced later in the evening.

It began with a thunderous rumble in Mom. Is the baby unhappy with the meal? Could they be rebelling for some reason? Dad, of course, provided no answers for poor Mom. Soon, the restroom rodeo began for her, Ralph, and Evelyn.

Mom began what some called "the green apple quick-step" to the bathroom. Ralph barreled from his bedroom to the bathroom, banging on the door. Panicked, he pried open the apartment door and ran as fast as his bulk allowed. At the bottom of the stairs, he plowed people over like a raging bull, making his way to the corner service station's men's room!

Evelyn followed Ralph's path, but Mom didn't give up her throne. Evelyn pleaded, but to no avail. Dad said nothing in the chaos. Trash stacked near the back door revealed an empty lard can, and Evelyn hastily grabbed it. In a flash, she slammed the door to her makeshift bathroom.

Dad got tickled by the scene but felt too bad to laugh. He faked something so the rest of the crew didn't get suspicious. He needed his best acting performance to date!

Mom left the bathroom, shaking and cussing about being pregnant, sick, and running for her life. Dad followed her in to pretend he'd gotten the same bug.

Dad gave adequate time in his "emergency" just as Evelyn crept from her room and bee-lined it to the bathroom. Ralph came into the apartment, eyes glazed, clutching his stomach. That bathroom door was closed again! He cussed, turned around, reopened the apartment door, and sprinted down the stairs like Jesse Owens!

Mom displayed anger and sickness all at once. Dad pretended, wondering aloud what had gotten them sick.

"You know, Emily, maybe it's the flu or somethin'! You hear about these kinds of things! I wonder if the meat went bad. Who knows where Ralph got it from?"

Mom agreed and decided that she and Evelyn would handle the marketing, since men wouldn't know a good piece of meat from a bad one. The bathroom game of musical chairs played out through the night in a symphony for the neighbors.

The "bug" miraculously left just as mysteriously as it appeared by the early hours of the next day. Ralph and Evelyn were wary of visiting family, but they went anyway. Mom and Dad needed time alone, but a required confession was coming. Deep teenage love came with testing!

Dad knew he needed to tell Mom the truth. He couldn't lie openly except as a prank or joke. He needed to come clean, and it wouldn't be easy.

"Emily, can I tell you something if you promise not to get mad, honey?" Dad inquired.

Mom, barely awake and wondering what hit her and the baby, had no time for games.

"Gus, if you got somethin' to say, well, then spit it out! I'm still tired since this poor child got kept awake all night, a-runnin' from somethin'!"

"Well, dear, I made a *small* mistake last night, uh, and I, uh, want you to know I'm sorry!" Dad mustered.

Now, he garnered Mom's full attention. She sat in bed and asked to look into Dad's eyes. She'd inherited something from Mamaw about interrogation. By her custom, she believed anyone who lied to her would have "devils in their eyes."

"What in tarnation are you tryin' to tell me, stupid man?" Mom barked.

"Well, I used the wrong salt in the potatoes last night! I kept salting and salting, and nothing happened. I searched around and realized I used Epsom salts instead!" Dad confessed.

"What? Mom screamed, You stupid, stupid man! Are you tryin' to kill us? Even the baby? Dummy, dummy, dummy!"

Mom grabbed a pillow and beat Dad's head with it as best she could. He sat there and took it, knowing he was at fault. When enough of the pounding occurred, she saw his smile, making her cuss, vowing revenge. He covered his face, and tears poured as he chuckled uncontrollably. Mom hadn't seen Dad laugh so hard.

"Emily, so help me, I uh, Hahahaha, I didn't know what to do! I couldn't tell anyone!"

Mom's anger turned to a smile, and then full-blown, new-love laughter took over her countenance. Both laughed into hysterics!

"Gus, I gotta tell you, hahaha, I ain't never seed a fat man move as ol' Ralph did! He went down those steps like a boxcar! I feel sorry for anyone standin' at the bottom. He'd a-flattened them, for sure!' Mom got out between giggles.

Dad held his side, giggling and kicking his feet. He caught his breath and went on talking.

"Evelyn came out and got that lard can, Emily! I swear, she got that lard can! I got tickled because it weighs more than she does! And Ralph down the steps, hahaha, like a linebacker, sheesh!"

It took years for fellow apartment dwellers to learn the truth. From this point forward, Dad's turn to cook rarely happened.

Dad acquired another talent that Mom knew nothing of, and its origin is still somewhat of a guarded family secret. In Dad's young life, he learned to flip his eyelids over. (For the record, he never taught his offspring how to do it, and we're thankful!) While it may seem a moot point or irrelevant, Mom found out the hard way in her newlywed status.

Mom welcomed Dad's routine of showering after eight long hours in a boiling hot bakery, but she did not anticipate how he would come out of the bathroom one day. He flipped his eyelids over, a gruesome sight to the uninitiated. Adding a zombie-like walk, Dad curled up his hands to attack. Moaning and groaning topped off the act as he approached his new bride.

Mom, for her part, prepped dinner and paid no attention. What idiot would surprise her in this late pregnancy? Only one! Dad sneaked up behind her, groaning and snarling as he got closer!

Mom, annoyed at first, ignored the noises. When she turned around, her face turned pale as she let out a thunderous scream! A monster entered her place! Yikes!

Dad chuckled and ran away with Mom in hot pursuit, spewing expletives as she went. Only a knock at the door from a concerned neighbor kept her from killing the father of her child. Dad's execution went on hold for the moment!

Mom explained her husband's stupidity, and Dad took a well-deserved "beating," laughing as he thrashed around. This pattern of behavior became normal for my parents. *Scaring* became part of living! God forbid someone tried to nap, for they had no chance of peace. A wooden spoon on an empty saucepan made an impromptu drum for the unsuspecting. "Experts in aggravation" made an excellent family crest.

A visit with family in Akron, too close to Mom's due date, came up, but the youngsters went without giving it a second thought. Mamaw watched as Mom had her first pains before asking everyone to time them.

Dad's nervousness increased as the pain came closer and closer. Papaw insisted on driving them to the hospital because Dad was in no condition to do it. A quick phone call put Akron General Hospital on notice to have a maternity crew on standby to deliver.

Mom and Dad got dropped off out front, and Mom fell into a waiting wheelchair. More uptight than ever, Dad looked for the father's waiting area and lit a smoke.

A few hours later, the glorious news of a baby girl born to the Stefanow family arrived! They named her Shirley, and both sets of grandparents rejoiced. After a few days in the hospital, mother and child returned to a cramped apartment. The small family needed a place of their very own.

Ralph and Evelyn threw a monkey wrench into Mom and Dad's plan for a new apartment by returning to Kentucky permanently one weekend, so they rushed to move. They could have been pickier, but found a place in their price range.

Dad re-entered the bakery plant field as a bread mixer again. The union job paid better than the first-shift work at the Akron bakery.

He got on with Fisher Baking on Lakeside Avenue, near the apartment. His short commute meant that he could almost come home for lunch.

Mom and baby Shirley settled in, and grandparents were frequent visitors. The adjustments began, and Dad wanted to avoid breaking his baby girl, which Mom *always* razzed him over.

Dad got the news at work that he'd get a new trainee to help. While young and ambitious, he trained anyone who intimidated him. He'd not been on the job long, and this didn't fall into his area of expertise.

He told Mom about what the boss asked him to do. Her response? "Train somebody, then!" It differed from what he wanted to hear as one of the newest people in the plant. Give his best and let the chips fall wherever they may. The pay and benefits were too good to dismiss.

Dad showed up at work for weeks for his early first-shift position. In the locker room, the usual banter went on. Guys talked about news, weather, sports, or women. Everyone went silent as Dad pushed open the door and walked to his locker. That's when the snickers and outright chuckles began.

"Man, this guy's been here a few months and already gettin' a trainee. Dummy!" laughed one smart-alecky coworker.

Ethnic and racial jokes were commonplace in the era. Raw language ruled the day in a workplace that was almost entirely male. The testosterone overload sometimes came to a boil. Dad let a few more cracks slide from the biggest mouth, but reached a limit.

Bigmouth railed on about Dad's ethnicity. He worked the crowd up, trying to split some sides before clocking in. He took a nasty turn when he mentioned certain ethnic women. Dad moved towards him and grabbed the floor with a few jokes.

"Why are there only two pallbearers at a 'certain ethnic' funeral? Because there are only two handles on a trash can!" Dad crowed.

Bigmouth couldn't get enough and asked Dad to please rattle off some more.

"Okay, buddy, why do they bury my people upside down in the graves? Huh?" Dad quizzed.

"Well, gee, I have no idea!" Bigmouth said.

Dad got a little closer and much, much louder with his answer.

"It's so people like you can kiss their butts!"

The insulted man tried to shove Dad into a locker, but other guys jumped in to defuse the situation. The profanity spewed thick and loud as the boss checked on the commotion. Everyone parted like the Red Sea and went to their machines.

Tensions amongst the men were nothing unusual. Each carried baggage in their own lives. Dad got a little more than he expected.

Just after lunch the same day, his foreman asked him to come to the office. Dad's heart sank as he contemplated his fate.

The foreman asked Dad to close the door. "Uh, this is it!" Dad thought. He wrestled with how he'd tell Mom what happened. A job loss meant ruin for the three of them. The foreman spoke up.

"Hey, look, I know guys spar every day in here over something. Someone has a bad night at home, or their kid gets into trouble, you know. I get that. So, I know what happened this morning, but I think you handled it well. You get a trainee tomorrow morning once he has filled out the insurance forms. Congratulations!"

Dad swallowed hard and extended his hand. The foreman shook it, opened the door, and gave Dad a friendly tap on his way out. He took a deep breath and decided the dinner discussion with Mom would be his golden opportunity.

CHAPTER SIX

Dad went out the door, eagerly following Mom's advice on the new trainee. He knew the mixer job was challenging for him when he first started. He needed to be kind and accept the person, regardless of their smarts or lack thereof.

Another day, "in the salt mines," the crew reminded each other. Hours into his shift again, the foreman stopped by his machine. Others asked if Dad liked being a "teacher's pet" or shop "mole' of some kind. The foreman greeted Dad with another request to close the door.

"Gusty, something dropped on me today, and I cannot let this happen without a heads-up! Nobody told me that, uh, this is how it is until the Personnel Director got me in his office. You need to know you are training a, uh, a, uh, Negro!"

Dad's shocked face said everything. He grew up in a lily-white area of Pennsylvania, where black people stopped in with car trouble. Deep inside, he knew that people were the same, but the other guys would laugh it up until Jesus came back! He delivered a devastating reply.

"Look, boss, I have no problem with anyone! I don't care if this guy is green, but these other punks aren't going to stop with making the job harder for this guy! I don't see it working out unless this guy has skin as thick as Larry Doby!" (The FIRST black American League baseball player.)

"Well, the foreman replied, "He's an ordained minister who preaches on the side. We both know he's going to need angels watchin' over him 'round here! Man, I'm clueless!"

Dad knew a couple of things. One meant that Bigmouth and others were not going for any perceived "forced" integration. Two, the new man would no doubt face direct racism that few, if any, of the whites would confront, even indirectly. Three, the rigors of the job were harsh enough without adding mental/emotional strains, too. Who would handle such an impending storm?

Both men found out when the new man knocked on the office door. Dad took a deep breath, nodded to the foreman, and opened the door—time for the niceties to begin.

Everyone introduced themselves in apparent awkwardness. The new guy impressively looked both his Caucasian friends right in the eye, adding a smile and a firm handshake. Things started well.

Dad took the new man to the locker room to suit up. Dad's questions needed answers.

"Hey, man, uh, what should we call you around here? I mean, is it Preacher, Padre, Minister, Parson, you know?"

A wide smile broke across the new guy's face. He knew Dad meant well, even if the stares on the floor from others did not.

"Oh, Parson, if you don't mind! Lots of folks call me that, so that will do fine!"

Dad heard a solid Southern drawl and asked where the man had been born. Dad told him he'd come from Pennsylvania coal country after the War.

Mr. Parson explained his Mississippi roots and lack of opportunity there. The Northern jobs came by the bushel, even for people of his skin tone. Cleveland looked like a promised land of sorts. He and his wife, Hettie Mae, wanted kids to pursue their American Dream. If he must be bi-vocational, then Mr. Parson embraced it.

The first day on the job proved more than Mr. Parson expected. *One* co-worker spoke to him as a fellow human being, a fellow sojourner to the grave. The man seemed an ally in a brave new world that had arrived.

The shift ended, and Mr. Parson followed Dad into the locker room. A reception awaited, but not a welcome wagon type. Hiring Mr. Parson opened eyes and mouths.

"Well, if it ain't my buddy and his Negro! Welcome in, fellas! Bigmouth said, sneering.

Dad stepped towards the man, but Mr. Parson moved before him, shook his head, and smiled. Dad's "justice complex" zoomed into high gear, and he never liked Bigmouth anyway. Mr. Parson was aware that he and Dad would get dismissed quicker than one could say Jackie Robinson lingered. Both men endured harassment every day. The long road together led to a close family friendship that lasted over five decades.

Dad ignored things until someone drew idiotic pictures and hung them on Parsons' locker. Dad's locker had words painted on it that expressed his perceived love of the black race in vivid, vulgar, racist terms. Mr. Parson pretended nothing happened, but Dad couldn't.

"Hey, you guys care when Marion Motley gets in the end zone for the Browns? Huh? You like Bill Willis crushin' people on defense? Yeah? Larry Doby smashes a home run, and you cheer, right? You know they're black, too? This man is tryin' to make a livin' like everyone else! Let's cut the crap!"

The room quieted for a moment when one jerk said he didn't care for black people. He didn't want to work with them or live by them. Dad asked more questions.

"Ever known any black people? No? Well, how do you know you can't stand them? This guy has taken your stupidity for months, and he's said nothing to make you hate him. He's Mr. Parson because he preaches every weekend! Where are the Christians here? Your Bible tells you to hate anyone, because mine doesn't! You watch, one day we'll elect a black president, and then what will you do? Move?"

Pandemonium swept the locker room as whoops and hollers, mixed with expletives and laughter, took over. A black president? Ha, the men chuckled.

Mr. Parson thanked Dad again for sticking up for him, but he wore down. The pay and benefits were great, but came at a high emotional and mental cost. Dad hatched a plan to cheer his new buddy up. Mom cooked a southern meal and invited them over.

Mom baked ham with the fixins for the two families. She made an upside-down pineapple cake for dessert and waited for the doorbell to ring. A Saturday at 6 p.m. seemed perfect. Dad interrupted Mom to help with the meal. *This time*, she controlled the kitchen.

The 6 p.m. bell rang on the small living room mantle clock, yet visitors still needed to arrive. Fifteen minutes later, Mom and Dad still waited. Mom urged Dad to run downstairs and find Parson.

It took about a minute to see Mr. Parson and his spouse sitting in a car out front. People were milling about, pointing, laughing, or taunting the frightened couple. Dad cleared the ignorant ones out and asked Mr. Parson to roll down the window.

"Hey, you guys comin' in? I mean, heck, you made it this far!" Dad asked.

"Man, you sure it's safe? Folks have been watchin' us since we pulled in! We kept the doors locked. Folks were going to cook us and eat us, Gus!"

"Oh no, they're just as stupid as the morons we work with. Come on now, Emily got the dinner cooked! And you get to see my Shirley, too!"

Dad led the way up the stairs as doors closed and locked, scared people peering out IF they dared!

Mom greeted the couple for dinner. She cooked too long and hard just for two. After introductions, Mr. Parson blessed the food. The simple prayer led to a dinner conversation.

Small talk commenced about the new baby, apartment, and life. Parson's wife, Hettie Mae, thanked Dad for helping her husband and standing up for him.

The meal ended, and Dad suggested he and Mr. Parson go for a walk. Hettie cautioned them due to the reception they'd gotten in front of the apartment. Dad said the ladies might get better acquainted with the men if the men were out of the way. Baby Shirley brought the wives together like nothing else.

Dad and Mr. Parson went downstairs and onto the streets of Cleveland. Mr. Parson warily walked beside Dad, aware that most people saw him in the wrong neighborhood. While nobody said anything out loud, the disgusted stares spoke clearly.

The two men rounded the corner to a pub Dad loved to frequent. Mr. Parson grabbed Dad by the shoulder to slow his advance.

"Man, look, I know none of my congregation is going to see me go in here, but these folks ain't going to like me comin' in! No, this seems like foolishness and I ain't much for takin' chances!"

Dad, the encourager who strived to see the good in others, convinced Mr. Parson to try it. Dad, the great salesman? Sure, years later, many claimed he'd be able to sell oil to the Arabs. Perhaps his charm overruled the objections of others. Regardless, things got interesting in the sleepy little pub.

Music played in the background as a bartender tended to his duties. The bar was nearly empty, but anticipation ran high among the clientele's "regulars" to appear after dark. Drinks were poured, as Saturdays were the most profitable, enough to keep the place open for the rest of the week.

The bartender watched as Dad bounced in, unable to see Mr. Parson's view. When he did, his face looked like it had consumed too many vinegar and lemon juice cocktails! To keep the other patrons happy, he refused Mr. Parson any service.

A few more would-be customers shuffled in, some watching in the shadows outside when Mr. Parson went in. They longed for entertainment on a dull Saturday night, and this fit the bill.

Dad's ninth-grade education meant he learned what he needed to know. His private study of human behavior proved no accident. He wanted to know what made others tick. There were never any unimportant people to him, whether in the checkout line, at the bank, or at the grocery store. He meant it when he'd throw a "How's life treatin' you" to the invisible masses! Did he want anyone's life story? No, but he wanted nobody overlooked. People responded well.

The bartender would not budge from his stance of serving only Dad. Mr. Parson glanced around the room towards the hateful stares, lowering his voice to tell Dad they needed to leave. Mr. Parson understood the situation far better than Dad did. Dad, ever the unpolished politician, spoke up!

"You people, you see this guy here? He's got two arms, two legs, and a head like every other joker in here! He works hard with me at the plant, and I'm treating him to a draft beer."

Patrons rose from chairs to surround the two "troublemakers" to intimidate them. Dad went back to his "sale" so everyone could hear.

"SO, this human being shouldn't enjoy a cold beer because your guys say he's a different color, right? Well...right? I say one thing to you: the only color around here that should matter is green, the color of cash! Now I say he's with me and he stays!"

Not one soul made another objection, and the bartender did the right thing. Dad and Mr. Parson didn't linger long, downing the beer, but were not about to be pushed out. Dad paid the tab, thanked everyone, and led Mr. Parson back to the apartment. Dad chalked up another story, but Mr. Parson wasn't keen about returning to the pub.

Back in the apartment, the wives got to know one another better. Both spoke of motherhood and its challenges, even though Hettie Mae had no children. Mom did her best to avoid her own mother's behavior and demeanor.

Neither man mentioned the problem at the bar for fear of hearing the wrath of the wives for going into it in the first place. Dad and Mom walked Mr.

Parson and Hettie Mae down to their car and said goodbye. A lovely first visit meant something special.

Back at the plant, the harassment slowed to a trickle as others grew more accustomed to a minority working alongside them. Dad, always one to liven up any situation (Dire or not), brought a bottle of vodka to work. He spiked the water cooler without anyone's knowledge. Dad poured the contents of the bottle of "spirits" into it to let the games begin. Harmless fun.

Dad got tickled just thinking about how much more the men would enjoy their work. He chuckled to himself as each soul took the altered H2O. He *did not* count Mr. Parson being the thirstiest guy on the shift!

Just before lunch, Dad checked on his buddy at his machine. He grew concerned when he didn't see him, but figured he had gone into the washroom.

Dad went into the locker room to grab his lunch, and Mr. Parson appeared passed out on a bench, completely gone! Dad tried waking him up before others came in to make snide remarks, but nothing worked. Thinking the heat was to blame, Dad and several sympathetic others rushed Mr. Parson into the showers, turning them on at full blast.

The shower's minimal success prompted the foreman to inspect his fallen employee. He agreed to let Mr. Parson lie on the bench until quitting time, but made Dad pledge to take him home.

The shift ended, and Dad, remorseful for a joke gone wrong, helped Mr. Parson to the backseat of the car. Mr. Parson seemed to come in and out of consciousness, babbling on about the Lord's glory, sights, wonders, and Judgment Day.

Dad got Mr. Parson into his apartment. He told Hettie that her husband might have heat sickness from the one-hundred-thirty-degree summer temperatures in the plant. Dad sprinted away while the lie hung in the air, trying to avoid eye contact. Hettie put Mr. Parson in bed and worried about her hard-headed man.

Dad got home later than Mom expected. As usual, he couldn't stop laughing when it hit him. Mom stood and listened.

"Emily, I did a stupid thing today!" Dad confessed.

"Well, why is it any different than any other day, huh?" Mom asked, sarcastically, whether she needed to trademark it because it had become her second language.

"You see, well, Mr. Parson and the water cooler, hahaha, I uh, well, you know that bottle of vodka I left over? I uh," Dad spouted out.

Mom interrupted with zero tolerance for what she'd already heard.

"No, no, you didn't, she screamed, Parson, a man of the cloth, too! Holy mackerel, Gusty, you got a *preacher* drunk? If you died and went straight to Hell, it would be your own fault. Just when you think you've seen dumb, well..."

Between snickers and chuckles, Dad did his best to confess his sin. He caught his breath to get it out.

"Emily, I swear, I had no idea he'd drink more from that cooler than anyone! So, help me, I didn't tell a soul what I did. It didn't seem to bother the other fellas!"

Mom wondered what kind of a man she had married. He could not be serious enough to save his own life. Things got worse when the phone rang.

Mom jumped up and grabbed the phone. Uh-oh, yes, Hettie Mae got worked up about her sick husband. Mom offered some advice, and, no doubt, she became known for it far and wide.

"Emily, Parsons' just a-layin' here moanin' and groanin' in our bed. He looks terrible, won't eat, and wants me to leave him alone. Said something about the heat at the plant...." Hettie spoke.

"Gee, Hettie, that's strange. Gusty said he took Mr. Parson home. He ain't going to tell you the truth because your man doesn't know what happened. Gusty told me the whole stupid story!" Mom bellowed.

"You see, Hettie, these grown men play pranks on each other, and Gusty is the ring-leader, for sure. He dumped vodka into the water cooler and let Mr. Parsons take what he wanted! My husband is the dumbest man in Ohio when it comes to pranks, I'm tellin' you!" Mom went on.

"So, my preacher man, you're tellin' me is nothing but blind-eyed, Emily, do I have this right? I've been a-babyin' his behind since he got home! Why, I'll go in that bedroom and roll that man out!" Hettie seethed.

"No, Hettie, don't do that to Parson! It ain't his fault! That blame goes to my dummy, Gusty, for actin' a-fool as he does! Oh, you know he got a piece of my mind for this stupidity!" Mom assured Hettie.

Dad took it in stride because playing jokes always came at a price. Some will get the humor, and others, well, not so much. Dad squared things with Mr. Parson and the foreman at the plant.

The next day, Mr. Parson waited in the locker room for Dad. Was he mad? Sure, but would he hold it against Dad forever? No way! Dad meant no cruelty. Mr. Parson mentioned that his paycheck would be short by four hours, and he needed ways to make up the shortfall.

Dad already felt terrible about his sin, but tried to offer solutions to make up for the money Mr. Parsons would miss out on. None of them seemed plausible. Mr. Parsons spoke.

"Gus, I ain't no drinker! The one beer's all I have in a year. I may drink a little wine sometimes, but man, the hard stuff is for other people. IF my congregation found out, some folks would not understand!"

Dad begged forgiveness over and over again, so Mr. Parson graciously accepted. While admirable, an apology would not fill his bank account. Dad, an above-average card player, offered a game to win some money back. Parson, already convicted of alcohol, disapproved of gambling. Dad acted on his own.

Dad didn't tell the foreman the truth about Parson's condition the day before. That stayed hidden for many reasons. Dad mentioned having a card party on Saturday night when his shift ended. How many suckers could he con with the lure of easy poker money? Payday Friday was no excuse for being left out, but the players needed cash to enter.

Papaw and Mamaw picked up Mom and Shirley to spend the night while the debauchery transformed the apartment into a saloon. Mom said, "Men, cold cuts, cigarettes, and gambling...can leave me out!" They'd be back Sunday afternoon to survey the damage.

Men crowded the place to maximum capacity. Mom made pre-cut finger foods and little sandwiches for the gamblers. The smart guys brought their own beer because they supplied only some of the crew.

Except for Dad's ribbing about his trainee and "pal" at work, the night went uneventful. The verbal jousting sharpened Dad's willpower to take money from the haters.

When it was said and done, Dad's winnings proved home-field advantage! He collected money from every player, including almost a dozen paychecks signed over. He'd cash them at his bank on Monday. His first call went to Parson, telling him he'd get his lost hours with Dad's help. Mr. Parson called it an answered prayer, no matter how it happened. Lady Luck did not like ugly!

Mom got home the next afternoon to a clean place, which said more about Dad's affections than anything. He and the fellows made a mess but cleaned up, too. Impressive! Even more surprises came when Dad handed his stack of cash and checks to his bride. He beamed with the joy of winning!

Mom thought about what to do with the loot, minus what went first to Mr. Parson and Hettie Mae. New furniture, always her priority, came next. Dad claimed for fifty-five years that Mom decorated each house with wall-to-wall furniture, and she didn't deny it.

Dad's glow of victory on Monday came with him to the plant. He pulled Mr. Parson aside and handed over cash for the lost hours from the random joke. He kept the uncashed checks at home, intending to deposit them after work. He smiled as wide as Lake Erie while others grimaced at him, aware that they were broke until payday. Taking their money gratified them beyond measure.

The day ended, and Mr. Parson thanked Dad again, but not in front of the losers from Saturday night. Dad had a spring in his step as he left the plant. Greenbacks were to pile up in his bank account! Dad celebrated the Second Christmas!

The atmosphere went from sunny and clear to stormy when Dad's feet hit the door's threshold. Mom stood there with Shirley in her arms, a look of total disgust on her face. Hurricane Emily queued up!

"Gus, you know how I spent my day? Huh? I tell you, it's Hell on earth, 'round here! Startin' at early this mornin', women have been a-bangin' on this door, a-cryin' like banshees over them lost paychecks you got! Some's got rent due, others got no groceries since their stupid men gambled everything away! More of them were cryin' away over the telephone, sayin' they don't know what to do!"

Dad wasn't taking this sitting down. He readied a defense as he scanned where he'd put the paychecks the day before.

"Emily, I swear I won every dollar fair and square! It ain't my fault they were dumb gamblers! They just got madder and madder every hand I won and went 'til they were busted flat!"

Mom pledged to give the checks back to the wives. She knew what it felt like to be destitute, broke, and hungry during the Depression. Dad looked at her like she'd grown a third eye. His ire shot up like a cruise missile in launch mode. He couldn't believe what he'd heard.

"Emily, you did what? I cannot believe it! You'd be that *stupid* with my money! Holy Christopher, I made plans for that cash! What is wrong with you?" Dad spewed in anger.

Dad fumed about "his" money and the prejudiced punks. He didn't even tell them he paid Mr. Parson for his lost hours. Mom wore him down on the "right thing to do" speech, and the uncashed checks returned to the previous owners.

Postwar prosperity soon came to a temporary halt. Border problems on the Korean Peninsula boiled over, affecting everyone in some way.

CHAPTER SEVEN

Just as Americans were getting accustomed to having the things that make life complete, an incident on the other side of the world ended everything. Thousands of communist North Korean troops rushed into South Korea.

American combat troops entered the fray on July 1st, 1950, and many feared the conflict would widen into a third World War.

Dad had tried joining the Navy during World War 2. Two older brothers were already serving, and he wanted to do his part at sixteen. He lied to a recruiter who diligently did his homework by talking to Mom Stefanow. She and Pop Stefanow allowed Dad to serve in the Merchant Marines. Luckily, the conflict ended in Japan, so Dad missed out.

The Korean conflict was something different. Americans served in a "police action" alongside other United Nations troops. If the U.S. instituted the draft again, it would take time to call up green draftees.

Dad pressed on with his bakery plant job, even looking into becoming a union steward when the slot became available. Mom worried herself sick about the war and the prospect of Dad going to the Far East. Dad's prime age for healthy young men meant no avoiding it. Mom had opinions.

"Gus, that ol' crazy Truman's got us in another war. I guess I don't understand all the politics, but I don't want you goin' off over there. That man has dropped an A-bomb on people, and he might use one again!"

Dad didn't fear military service and would do his best. His worries about his family were at the forefront of his mind.

"Emily, we've got no say in the matter! You can't run, now, can you? I mean, everybody has to do their part. So, if they draft me, they draft me." Dad assured himself as he convinced himself.

Mom couldn't see herself raising Shirley on her own. She'd move in with her folks and lose the apartment altogether. She had the option to move in with her in-laws. Adding in Shirley helped, but Mamaw might have a fit over it. Mom envisioned no sense in a war in any way, shape, or form.

"Gus, don't it seem like rich men start these wars, but poor men fight them? I don't understand what'll make one human kill another!"

Dad was not interested in making sense of the international scene. His focus was on being a good husband and father.

"Emily, the world's always been a tough place for the average working man, and it always will be! We got no clout, no money, and no understanding of such things. We're too busy livin' each day."

Parson had some understanding of what he and Dad should do about an impending draft notice for each of them. He called Dad with the plan.

"Gus, you see, I've been thinkin' on all this war stuff. I'm going to go down and volunteer for the Chaplain Corps! You can join me down there and tell them you're a baker, first-class. Now with integration, we can get trainin' together. Maybe neither of us will go to the front lines! I just don't cotton to bullets and bombs! Cleveland's dangerous enough!"

Dad appreciated all the thought his buddy put into both of them. He could not see himself signing up ahead of time, though. What about taking chances with the draft numbers? Maybe nobody calls them at all. Dad had a gambling streak in him his whole life.

Both men got draft notices months later and did what they had to do. The waiting game grated on them as friends and co-workers wondered about the future daily. Life and the uncertainties it held were ordinary for everyone. The prospect of war puts one's thoughts aside and is always at the forefront of the mind.

Time marched on, and again, Mom's calendar told a tale about a coming stork. Mom knew she was pregnant, and she wasted little time telling everyone. Little Shirley would be two and a half when her play partner arrived. This time, there'd be no surprises as with a first child. However, the pregnancy differed in delivery.

Dad again paced the floor of the local hospital, smoking like the proverbial chimney. This time, he had the company of his in-laws, parents, and Parson. A delivery delayed due to the baby's positioning meant swift work by the doctor's staff to keep the mother and child alive. The hours dragged on, but another baby girl appeared in the nursery! Dad and Mom could not have been prouder. They named their newest little girl Linda. Shirley got herself a playmate.

Dad got the union steward position at work that he had been wanting. He kept his job at the oven and dealt with labor and management issues. Dad didn't care for being the "complaint department," as some viewed it. He explained why the steward set the pace for other employees, exasperating Dad. Dad told everyone that stewards come to work on time, take appropriate lunches/breaks, and clock out as required. They were the *example*. He believed in an honest day's work for fair pay. No tolerance for laziness occurred on Dad's watch. Those who didn't work hard got dismissed- <u>no</u> exceptions.

Neither Dad nor Parson had to attend as the Korean War wound down. Inflation ran high during the war, driving up prices and wages. Once the war ended, a recession not seen since the Great Depression complicated things for everybody.

Cutbacks on overtime at the plant meant fewer paychecks. Layoffs came and went. Linda's first Christmas, 1952, settled as a tough one. With twelve dollars to their names, Dad insisted they put something under the tree for Shirley, at the very least. A trip to Sears and Roebuck netted them a shiny new tricycle, but nothing more. (This spending pattern started a foundational habit for their lifetime. Buy now, *think* later.) They awoke Christmas morning to one pound of bacon in the refrigerator for the feast. Hard times had come, but hope said they didn't last. Pride wouldn't allow them to share their circumstances with their parents. No way.

Mom and Dad's apartment got crowded with the new baby and the accessories they required. With help from Parson and Hettie Mae, they moved to a roomier place. Dad got promoted to foreman, and the families rejoiced. The 1950s were fruitful in many ways.

Dad's legendary love of family meant frequent trips to Pennsylvania and Kentucky. A christening or wedding often united the young travelers, but death united them.

Dad's Uncle Joe had a bulbous, reddish nose and a penchant for strong drink, which led to hilarious stories about the family in the Old Country. Dad sat and listened for hours. When Uncle Joe, Dad's favorite, passed away unexpectedly, the family jumped onto the Pennsylvania Turnpike to take advantage of the superhighway.

A six-hour drive from Cleveland, Dad arrived at Aunt Mary and Uncle Gene's place in Hazelton, PA. Hugs and tears filled the room, and everyone marveled at Shirley and Linda. The youngsters lightened the solemn occasion.

The service went well the next day and afterward at the church. Dad told stories all evening at Aunt Mary's about Uncle Joe. The man once claimed a ghoul popped out of a cemetery on his way home from a local bar. Uncle Joe ignored the little creature, but when the ghoul wanted to fight, Uncle Joe obliged and beat its face in. He felt so bad that he went to the cops to report his deed. The cops came back to the cemetery to find no one there. They threatened to arrest Uncle Joe for public intoxication. Tales like these went on for hours.

As the night faded, Mom, Dad, and the girls settled on couches and the floor. Dad chuckled with Mom a little more before falling into a deep sleep. He dreamed of Uncle Joe and the fun they'd had together.

Aunt Mary's dog loved a blanketed floor with a pair of warm bodies. The poor animal had a busy day with the family in for the funeral. He was a part of the family, so he entered the dozing couple's presence.

The dog wiggled and writhed into a small space between Mom and Dad, snuggling. The household shook and awakened when the cold, wet nose touched Dad's face!

Dad sprang up from the covers, screaming about Uncle Joe getting him! He ran in place, then in circles, as the lights came on and the bedroom doors opened. Angry sleepers arose to see what the commotion was!

"Jesus, Mary, and Joseph, I swear Uncle Joe had me! I'm dreamin' about him, and then he stuck his big, cold nose to my face! I had to run!" Dad stammered.

Aunt Mary surveyed the living room and smiled as others threw up their hands in disgust, muttering expletives about getting no rest.

"Gusty, Uncle Joe is *dead* and gone! You scared the bejesus out of my dog! He loves to snuggle up, you big chicken!" Aunt Mary said, laughing as she went back to bed.

Dad laughed at himself, thinking that if it were Uncle Joe, he'd have wanted Dad to dress and head with him to his favorite bar. A return to Ohio came in the morning.

Back to the daily grind at home, Dad zipped through the traffic after work for a shower, a good meal, and time with his sweet angels. Mom had other plans.

Mom has been called "vertically challenged" due to her five-foot stature. She made do with heights that were out of her reach.

Dad hugged her and his girls as he surveyed the packages on the dining table. Mom cheered his arrival for many reasons.

"Gus, help me get these curtains up in the kitchen and living room. I've been waitin' all day!"

Dad, reeking of the inescapable bakery plant heat, insisted on a shower first. He was always glad to help, but he had his priorities.

As Dad showered, Mom used a dining chair as an impromptu stepladder out of impatience. Mom didn't mind waiting on anyone as long as they acted in *her* time. That fact drilled itself home religiously and daily.

Dad dressed and exited the bathroom. With a swing in his step, he hugged his girls and tickled them under their necks in their bedroom. Mom waited impatiently!

Dad hopped into the living room, and his jaw dropped.

"Holy Christopher, Emily, are you trying to kill yourself? I can't raise these girls by myself! What are you doing?" Dad screamed.

Mom had gotten up on the chair, stretching herself to eyeball the curtain bracket, as dangerous footing displayed.

"Gus, take it back! Take it back, one-two-three-four-five! Take it back, silly man, take it back!" Mom shouted back.

Dad looked at Mom like she'd lost her mind. Take what back? Count? Why? What a bizarre request!

"I said take it back, you know, about me a-dyin' over here! I ain't dyin', not today! Don't be jinxin' me!" Mom replied.

Dad stood there bewildered. How could he jinx her? Mom's hybrid Christianity-superstition mixture came into play all the time.

"Alright, alright! I take it back one-two-three-four-five! Miserable woman! Holy Christopher, I take it back! Look at where you're standing!" Dad replied.

Mom and Dad both learned that marital bliss comes at a cost.

A freak accident at work reduced the progress toward the American Dream. In moving a hopper full of one ton of dough, a wheel got lodged in a rut in the flooring. Without asking for help, Dad pushed and shoved with all his might. In an instant, he blew out several disks in his spine.

In the late 1950s, medical advances in treating back injuries were minimal. After some rest and X-rays, Dad's doctor recommended a surgeon to "fix" the problem. A spinal fusion involves removing bone from a hip and squaring off the removed disk(s). After months of recovery, the surgeon cleared Dad to return to work.

In the meantime, Mom got herself a job in a paint factory, not wanting Dad to rush back and feeling the need to contribute. She lasted about a week, adding lids to cans with a mallet. A chemical in the paint caused her skin to break out in a rash, so she moved to a different role.

Mom sat down at a machine, with greasy parts coming at her on an assembly line. Oil sprayed into her face with each passing article. She'd inspect, wipe her brow, and then see how many pieces piled up on her—a week on the line convinced her to go back to waitressing and getting by on tips.

Dad healed and went back to work. The surgery was the first of many and haunted him in his adult life. The temporary fix offered minimal relief at best.

As the 1950s wound down, changes mounted. Mom and Pop Stefanow moved back to Pennsylvania for their sunset years. It meant back to the Ohio and Pennsylvania Turnpikes for the youngsters with the kids in tow to Hazelton. Mom and Dad celebrated their tenth wedding anniversary with Parson and Hettie Mae before peering into the 1960s. A new decade led to family expansion, offset by two life-altering losses.

CHAPTER EIGHT

The sixties arrived with the inevitable effects of time. Pop Stefanow passed away in March 1960 after a long illness. Dad's hero and mentor's passing left an enormous hole in the family. Pop spoke little, but years after Dad married Mom, he asked Dad to take him for a ride. Once at a local park, Pop told Dad that his woman was one in a million! He loved Mom and encouraged Dad to care for her and his girls.

Dad got back to Hazelton many times after to check on Mom Stefanow. He once took her to the grocery store, and when she counted her change on the way back, the clerk overpaid her by one cent. She made Dad take the penny back halfway across town in her usual style. Everyone adored her honesty and decent living.

In mid-October 1961, Dad got word that his mom had taken a turn with worsening health, so he and the family drove back to Hazelton. Although not wholly better, Dad returned home.

Back in Cleveland, Dad unloaded the car trunk, which held many suitcases. While lugging some inside, the telephone rang, and Dad answered it. With a gulp and tears, he told the family that Mom Stefanow had just passed. Everyone got back into the car, gas purchased, and then went back to the Turnpike for another funeral.

Doctors blamed heart problems for Mom Stefanow's death, and the whole family knew it was true. Thirty-five years together in a legendary love meant that Mom Stefanow died from a broken heart. She and Pop Stefanow were content to hold hands and enjoy each other's company anywhere. Dad shook to his core to lose both parents so swiftly. These losses he never came to grips with his entire life.

Dad became a patriarch at the ripe old age of thirty-two. His relationship and reliance on his parents' wit, wisdom, and leadership were taken away in a short eighteen-month span. How could he cope? He reluctantly moved forward with his wife and preteen girls. He seemed a lost sheep.

Mom prayed for years for sons. Dad, even if he couldn't admit it, did too. The usual things came into play, such as passing a name on or mentoring a male to mold into the next Stefanow man. The Lord answered Mom's prayer in October 1963. I entered the world with fanfare, but could only pass the information as reported. As Mom always said, "The world needed a Big Gus and Little Gus," so I came along just in time.

My reign as king of the Stefanow world lasted about two years. I have no recollection of it, but it must have been nice. There are photos and videos of me stalking the New York World's Fair in 1964, probably looking at the Ford Mustang! Both sisters took turns spoiling me, and then, out of nowhere, my little brother Felipe (Phil) provided spite work just by showing up. He became an accomplice, confidante, and scapegoat. Nobody got a better partner-in-crime than me!

Dad's old back injury reared its ugly head after Phil came along in 1966. Scar tissue had built up for a decade and reached the point of debilitation. Dad could not ignore it and set a date to see Dr. Arnold at the Cleveland Clinic. Mom distrusted medicine, which rolled from her tongue like butter on a hot biscuit.

"Gus, that ol' quack is why you're hurtin' now! And you, a man with brains, go back again? Lord, you don't make any sense! You might be better off with an animal doctor this time!" Mom squealed.

"Emily, I gotta do somethin' here! If it doesn't get done, I'll get worse! You hate medicine and doctors, but I can't take chances. We gotta eat, and I gotta work!" Dad responded.

Mom, less than thrilled, knew carrying on the conversation would go nowhere. Months of struggle lay ahead.

Once Dad had overcome the economic hardship of being out of work for months, his workaholic superhero persona kicked in. He and Mom believed traveling promoted a healthy part of the American Dream.

The Stefanow family vacations were legendary. Dad busted his behind working overtime for extra money. Other times, he'd get bonuses and take us somewhere we wanted to go. Mom picked up waitressing to set money aside, too. We traveled more than most of my friends. Each time, an adventure came up.

Linda and Shirley were excited and picked Florida's Busch Gardens for one trip. We were having a ball until we crammed into a motel room. Mom performed her usual pre-lodging inspection, and the place passed. We swam and ordered room service, as we sometimes did. By nightfall, we passed out from near exhaustion. I crammed into a bed with my older sisters, as always. I tried sleeping, but something grazed my ear and made it itch. My scratching kept my weary sisters from sleeping. In frustration, Linda bolted out of bed and turned on the light. When she did, we saw the walls covered in insects that looked like cockroaches to our Ohio eyes. Mom lit off from the bed like a jackrabbit, shrieking and struggling while removing blankets. Both sisters were in on the act while Dad flailed around to find his pants. We batted the flying monsters and left, grabbing what we could. Dad went to the office for a refund and restoration of his eardrums. Incensed, he opened the car door.

Holy Mackerel, he said, they say these bugs are normal here. Guess they're palm bugs of some kind. I got our money back, and we'll go somewhere else, kids!"

Mom chimed in, of course.

"Call them what you will, Gus, but they're flyin' roaches to me! Them things have got wings! No way am I stayin' anywhere with flying cockroaches!" Mom's mental state brought excitement, but bugs in our room topped it.

We found more suitable lodging and tumbled in. The next day, we spent at Busch Gardens, a glorious experience with one exception.

We anticipated hot, humid weather beforehand. Nature filled the scene with bright birds, seals, wild animals, and fountains. When we got a glorious shade on a trail, Mom's athletic ability showed itself again!

Taking a breather from the heat and humidity in the shade proved priceless. Mom constantly reminded us that she once had a heat stroke down South, which made her run around insane. We took comfort in the brief recess.

Dad rounded up the troops, and we marched forward, with Mom bringing up the rear. We scanned the beautiful trees and colors. Then, at once, Mom let out a shriek that could've curled hair! Everyone turned around as a white streak, wearing a floppy hat, zipped past us. Mom ran at warp speed for reasons unknown. Everyone heard "Sssssssnnnnnake! Snake!"

Mom left our entire party in the dust. Dad shook his head, cussed, and rounded us back up again. He looked further behind us as other guests slowed their pace. A colossal snake of unknown variety fell out of a tree and landed at Mom's feet! She passed us faster than Speedy Gonzalez, but we caught her in the gift shop, shaking and in an uproar.

In the end, the adults got a beer on their way out. Mom sprinted to the car, heat notwithstanding, and turned on the engine for the air conditioning. We went back home as quickly as possible.

Mom and Dad moved us into a rental house in Euclid just as my sisters became teenagers. Both parents knew the need for safe places for the younger generation to gather. Dad's youth was full of turmoil and truancy. Mom's well-documented runaways and strict discipline were ineffective. When our family pediatrician suggested Dad consider teen dances, the idea stuck. Dad acted because much of the future awaited us.

Euclid had small shops and local hangouts, but not a place where the young danced and mingled. Community service invaded my parents' wheelhouse. The kids needed a common area and were determined to get one for *everybody*. My parents stepped out on faith and got something going.

Where does one start to organize something of community value that benefits the teenagers of any society? Dad and Mom thought the Euclid City Council was the linchpin in the plan. The council welcomed it but with caution. Where would they hold dances to attract hundreds of teens on weekends?

Dad believed that churches should be places that drew folks to faith *and* fun. He thought we should express our joy in ways that made Christianity attractive and relevant. He extended grace to believers and unbelievers alike. Saint Anthony's parish had a hall perfect for the project, so Dad met with the leadership to procure the facility.

The church board reinforced the city council's concerns. Yes, the community dances were excellent for teens, but questions arose. How late will the dances run? Who will be the chaperones? Will security be available? The objections mounted, but Dad got answers.

Dad and Mom got a permit from the city of Euclid, albeit with reservations. Dad set off-duty police onsite, selected dates and hours, and reported to the city council as required. The church wanted a weekly cleanup of the facility and meetings to review the agreement. Things were moving!

Dad found a vendor willing to supply soft drinks and snacks on consignment. He also worked with a local grocery chain to provide hot dogs, buns, and other supplies for hungry teens. He hired the meanest bouncer he could find, a fellow who chewed on a water glass when irritated. Smart people left the man alone.

Lest anyone forget, Dad was still working full-time when the planning happened. He needed to hire bands and required more time for auditions. Word of mouth spread, and if the bands stank up the place, the kids let him know.

Word got out in the community that the dances were on Friday nights, well chaperoned, and had appropriate security to alleviate adult fears.

When Opening Night came, hall overcrowding meant that kids got in only after others left. Angry potential patrons were waiting in long lines outside, but most understood.

Mom and Dad hadn't anticipated the hordes of teens coming to OUR house after dancing the night away! Dad himself had cleanup duties and accounting to do after closing. The dance idea was successful, but pizza, soft drinks, and snacks afterward at the Stefanow house had not yet been factored in. Regardless, my folks were happy to provide a safe place for kids.

My earliest remembrances of this timeframe have our home being like a Greyhound bus terminal. I saw big people everywhere, smiling and laughing. Sometimes, I crimped language when I entered a room, and conversations stopped. I never knew why until much later. Music always played on a stereo or two at our house. Naumann Avenue in Euclid became the "in-crowd" of the day. We had our very own "Laugh-In" set on the premises.

Our doorbell rang one afternoon when Dad, Phil, and I were there. Dad yelled for me to look out to see who was beating on our door. I peeled back the curtain for the surprise of my life when I saw black boots, a black jacket, and a black hat on the largest brown giant in America! I ran to the living room, where Dad struggled to put a new diaper on Phil.

"Daddy, daddy, there's a brown giant out there, like Parson, but soooooooooo big! He got a black hat on, and he, uh, he's a giant!

Dad slipped one leg over my squirming brother, finished the last diaper pin, put Phil in the playpen, and moved from the couch to the front door. I stood behind him, proud of my discovery, getting his attention.

"Oh, Jesus, Christopher, Junior! He's my friend, Otis! Otis Johnson, come on in! Dad exclaimed as he let the giant inside.

I marveled at the giant's stature, unsure if our ceilings might accommodate his height. Dad led him into the kitchen, the giant ducking under the arched doorway. Dad then produced two brown bottles of beer for each to enjoy. I stared at the giant's bottle as it disappeared into humongous hands.

This brown giant differed from our friend Mr. Parson because he hadn't spoken much. He never once tried chasing me down and baptizing me. He listened to Dad, then let out a booming laugh that echoed through the kitchen and throughout the house. I heard from the living room when he talked, out of eyesight.

"Huh, Hahahaha! Gusty, when you told me that story about Mr. Parson gettin' drunk...man, you killed me! Huh, Hahahaha!" Otis blurted out.

The giant's chuckles made me snicker, and then I got revealed! Dad told me to come to the kitchen and meet Otis face-to-face.

I walked in slowly, carrying my Lone Ranger hat, mask, and six-gun belt, which I needed help to buckle. (Phil became Tonto but didn't know it yet.) Otis reached out his hand to shake my tiny one. I could have hidden in one of the man's boots! His monstrous paws eclipsed my whole hand and half my arm.

Dad put the ensemble on me and explained my Lone Ranger fixation. Otis told me they always needed a good man at the plant, even when I was young. I sat beside Dad and got overwhelmed by the giant. They drank a few more brews, and Otis left on a big, loud motorcycle in a flash.

Dad took Phil out of the playpen while I ran around shooting at imaginary bad guys. The telephone rang as soon as Otis cleared our street. Our next-door neighbor, known as Porky Pig, broke down on the line because of his stuttering.

Dad listened for a moment or two before interjecting. The neighbor was hysterical as Dad spoke.

"Hey, hey now! No, I'm not sending that big guy to your house! No, no! He works with me at the plant!" Dad answered.

Dad rolled his eyes as the man raved about being a better neighbor.

"Look...look, who I have over here is my business, get me? Gee, I didn't notice him being black. And you're going to be nicer to my kids, huh? Okay then. No, I won't send him or any others over to hurt you. It's settled!" Dad replied. He chuckled when he set the phone down. One problem resolved itself.

The dances at St. Anthony's Hall made headlines, but only sometimes, the kind my parents wanted. Most citizens supported establishing a place where young people could hang out for a few hours without getting into trouble. Others questioned the teenage attire, the slow dancing, or reports of fights before and after the event. Dad fought for the permits that kept the dances going.

One late night after cleanup, a group of guys approached Dad about taking a ride with them. They were kids of good standing within the community. Even in adulthood, Dad, ever the "Little Rascal," agreed to see around town.

The ride proved short but passed through neighborhoods Dad knew very well. The driver pulled the car over and told Dad about a high school teacher who was giving him and the gang a hard time over their grades. The teacher demeaned the pupils, and that got Dad interested.

When four young men testified, Dad received a hubcap chock full of rusty lug nuts. They parked in front of the teacher's home, thinking *someone* should teach the guy a lesson by busting the home's picture window. Delighted, Dad crept out of the car with his weapons.

The breaking glass almost raised the dead as Dad hustled to the getaway car. Mission accomplished! Moments later, with Dad and the boys at our house, sirens pierced the serenity of the night. Soon, the vandals surveyed their damage as "concerned citizens" and drove past the crime scene.

Cops were everywhere. Flashing lights blinded the line of passersby, eagerly viewing the damage. Dad sat in the passenger seat as the car slowed to speak with an officer.

"Hey, what happened here, buddy?" Dad inquired.

"Well, Gusty, some punks smashed a picture window out. A poor widow lay in bed asleep. What's the world comin' to, huh?" The officer asked.

Dad shook his head while the driver moved slowly. The guys were silent as they realized they'd targeted the *wrong* house. There'd be Hell to pay if Mom found Dad the culprit. He did not tell her, but everybody agreed they'd pay for the window replacement. No more pranks, Dad insisted as they got back home. One rotten teacher lucked out that night.

The dance sensation came under such scrutiny that my family could not contain it. The "79th Street Gang" members caused havoc in and around each dance. The community worried about teen safety and keeping up appearances. No recourse was available, so the dance cards played themselves out.

Promising young men visited our home before shipping off to a place everyone called "V-et-Nam." Many of my sister's classmates never returned, and chaos and protests about the war were beginning.

The assassinations of Bobby Kennedy and Martin Luther King caused violent eruptions nationwide. Armored personnel carriers rolling through Euclid and Cleveland in the late 1960s pressed my folks into moving a little east. Our first home, owned on Alva Drive in Eastlake, was our family homestead for three decades.

While the new house needed more than a facelift, it became the "party place" of the neighborhood. We hosted anything from a simple summer bash to a Lawn Jart championship Dad won yearly. Seventies style settled in.

CHAPTER NINE

The Sixties came and went in a flash. The promise of the Seventies, in a rehabilitated home with newfound wealth, made every challenge worthwhile. Linda married off soon after we moved in, and Shirley followed. Optimism ruled the days in our fresh surroundings.

The house was the worst one in the best possible neighborhood. Although just three years old, it resembled the Munster house. After months of evening work, Dad and my uncle Jim Crazie made the inside inhabitable again.

The yard itself looked as if trench warfare had been fought there. We were on a dead-end street (Something always bothered Mom about the sign announcing it.) right beside a ditch filled with vile mosquitoes, trash, and creepy-crawlies of all kinds. It took several years for the city to fill the canal and end the neighborhood aberration.

My parents believed in the value of vacations, deeming them a part of the American Dream. Besides obligatory runs to Pennsylvania and Kentucky, we went all over the United States. Mom wanted to see faraway places, perhaps because Dad drove most of the time. Mom told the world that the only flying she'd do would mean meeting Jesus one day. So, we used the family truckster or borrowed Papaw's station wagon if needed. Our first trip from the Eastlake homestead took us to Dallas, Texas. Air conditioning or not, off we went in our '68 Chevy Caprice.

Dad took the wheel, and we sped from the driveway hours after the planned "early" start. My folks took enough clothes to start their second-hand store anywhere along the line. We'd travel a hundred miles before Mom developed a "hungry-sick" problem called "hangry" by folks today. An unsanitary truck stop got our drinks, pretzels, chips, and exposure to hepatitis as a bonus. We partied and took chances.

Dad took being a self-made man to the extreme by *never* bringing any maps. He just read the interstate signs and hoped for the best. A forward thinker, he exhibited no identity crisis within his manhood by asking for directions! We headed to Uncle Tommy's house, Dad's mustachioed twin. No estimated arrival time came from Dad's lips when we went on a trip. Dad knew better.

Things were good for us through the Midwest and into Saint Louis, Missouri. We stopped at the arch and looked around. Mom stayed behind as Dad, Phil, and I took the elevator to the top. Heights? Yep, Mom feared them, too. Back in the car after a lunch break, we entered Oklahoma.

The Missouri heat had been alright on the old Chevy. However, we hit an invisible wall of pure warmth in Oklahoma. Mom and Dad were always smart enough to get seat covers with two active little boys, but the intense heat made them feel like we were sitting on a hot griddle. Worse than that, I fell asleep and awoke with thousands of red dots on my face. I looked like I got the 'pox again. Oh, I played it up well enough to make Mom think about getting me into the nearest hospital. When I confessed to the seat cover gag, I nearly got "crowned" king of the road!

We arrived at Uncle Tommy's place in the late afternoon, days later. To keep Phil and me busy on the trip, Mom gave us crayons and coloring books for the back seat. Once we stopped, she asked for them back for safekeeping. I learned a lot about crayons and 110 degrees of heat that day. Dad never let us forget it.

Hours later, after the newness of our arrival wore off, we went to an authentic Texas steakhouse! Uncle Tommy said one could almost pick out the steer in the corral out back. We were ready!

Phil and I raced to the old Chevy and waited for Dad to unlock it. Mom opened the passenger door and hesitated. It might have been more than one hundred fifty degrees inside with all the windows up! Regardless of the temperature, Mom inadvertently left the *entire* box of Crayola crayons on the dashboard.

Dad opened his door and glanced at the dashboard not once but twice! The crayons had gotten hot, becoming a colorful cauldron, melting up and out of the box. The black dashboard revealed a menagerie of said colors about eight inches high. To make it worse, the dripping from the box covered the heat/defrost and vent controls. Dad stepped away from the car as he accosted his beloved.

"Hey Emily! Jesus, Mary, and Joseph, you set those crayons on there?" He asked.

As we stood there, a deafening, Texas-sized silence encompassed us. Uncle Tom and Aunt Mary Ann were busy getting my cousins, Nick and Parris, into their car so they might miss the confrontation. Wrong!

Mom mustered enough to say she didn't think she'd set them in a dumb place. With getting Phil and me out, well, Dad didn't hold back. The long drive took its toll on him, and the heat in a car without air conditioning didn't help. He questioned his brainpower about buying a car like that, but many lived without the A/C in Cleveland.

"How you did this, I dunno. I'm busy drivin', it's hot as Hell out there, and you leave crayons on the dash. Aye, miserable woman!" Dad lamented.

Uncle Tom, Dad's near clone, looked at the car, snickered, and made a quick decision about a butter knife. He scurried back into the house, cussing as he went about stupidity. He gave the butter knife to Dad, who cursed about the mess. Before long, we were eating red meat, Texas-style!

We visited Six Flags amusement park and enjoyed the family, which was very important to Dad. We drove all night to avoid the Texas heat. (And no crayons in sight!) Dad's successes were his coffee, cigarettes, and caffeine in the soft drinks he kept in a cooler. Back to Fortress Eastlake!

Once home on Alva Drive, we got the bad news that Mom's Uncle Hoss died in Akron the next day. We dressed for a "wake," and I knew no deceased couldn't be awake. My first funeral came up.

I was still determining what to expect at Uncle Hoss' place. We went down a long hallway, snaking through the kitchen to the back of the house. A large brown wooden box rested right in front of us. Mom and Dad stood there, paying respects. Phil took off to play, but I got on my tiptoes to see a man lying there. I watched a fly dance across his forehead, then take a peek up his nose before zipping to greener pastures. Dead as last week's pot roast—no doubt!

Mom stood there in a trance-like state as she stared into the casket. Dad grabbed her arm to pull her away, and then, to our surprise, she ran away, gagging in an "Eck, eck, eck, eck" style she performed. Dad followed her out.

"Gus, oh, Gus, he spoke to me! Uncle Hoss spoke to me, I tell you! Right there in that room, the man spoke!" Mom revealed.

Dad and I heard nothing. Nobody heard anything but Mom. Dad nodded and said we should get back home as soon as possible. None of us realized the long road ahead with Mom's mental state.

The incident at Thanksgiving, 1971, became well-known within the family. Mom limped into the house to keep from freezing to death in front of the yard statues of Mary and Jesus. Mom's doctor, Simmons, helped her with her behavior. Her abnormal fixation with all things death remained. Doctor Simmons reminded her that the breakdown resulted from an upbringing by Mamaw that left permanent scars. We coped collectively before another setback came along.

About a year after the first diagnosed breakdown, Mom suffered another. She took her medicine and visited Dr. Simmons. With my grandparents in Kentucky and Dad working double shifts in his management job at New York Frozen Foods, Mom snapped again, much harder. Out of her mind, despite the best help available, she leaned on Shirley. She called at all hours, which didn't sit well with my new brother-in-law. He never complained, but I know it bugged him when Mom called 24-7.

Mom went from being managed to a dangerous situation in which she walked between our house doorways, never taking more than a step in each direction. Her eyes rolled back in her head as she mumbled gibberish and counted on her fingers. The bizarre sight gave way to a state of mind far worse than imagined. Dad brought out the heavy artillery!

Dad didn't know what to do with Mom. He called priests from our local parish, and each prayed with Mom, but it didn't help much. Mom called in her local Baptist minister, Pastor Heller, who prayed over her each time. He assured her of her place in Heaven, but even that didn't calm her fears.

We went to a psychic healer in Pennsylvania who proclaimed Mom under a spell. After cleaning Mom with sage, he gave us a bag of salt to spread on each exterior door. We were desperate!

One night, Dad waited for Mom to pick him up at the plant. Phil and I jumped into our old Dodge Dart as Mom adjusted the seat before take-off. We were eager to see Dad after a long day with Mom.

Mom fired up the engine and backed down the driveway. We went three houses up our street before a large black cat dashed across our path. Mom hit the brakes, sending Phil and me onto the floorboard. Mom's face turned a pasty white as she faced us both.

"Well, kids, you know what this means!" Mom screeched.

Yes, we knew what it meant. Mom made up superstitions as she went along. We'd wait until some other sap drove by, allowing the bad luck to fall onto them. Mom sat in front of our neighbor's house and waited. We amplified the not-so-perfect tonic for two fidgety young boys on a hot summer night.

"Uh, Mom, I piped up, do you realize how *long* we will sit here before someone comes behind us?"

"Yes, Junior, I realize that, you know I do! Mom snapped back. We'll wait!"

I made several more attempts to reason with Mom, but got nowhere. Heck, Phil and I wanted to go to the house. I knew Dad would be incensed, and rightfully so.

We sat in our automotive prison. With each car that came down the street, we got the sensation that a shipwrecked sailor must get when seeing a vessel on the horizon. It came near but then faded away. As each car found a driveway, our hopes dropped.

Mom bristled at the car approaching us as I dozed off in the darkness. She cheered as it glided past our old Dodge and into a driveway. She turned the key on and shifted into first gear. We were off!

We had a good time as Mom drove faster than usual. I couldn't figure out how it helped, but I kept my mouth closed. We skirted into the factory parking lot in a rush. Phil and I waited in the car as Mom hustled to find dear old Dad. We both sensed an actual test of their marital bliss. It was time!

Mom double-timed a move out the shop doors in minutes with Dad in hot pursuit. Under the parking lot lights, his face appeared as red as the car we were driving. He breathed murderous threats toward Mom and spouted fire out of both ears. His language peppered the night sky with unprintable expletives.

"Holy mackerel, Emily," Dad roared, "You even have these poor kids in the car, too!" He jerked the door handle open and plopped into the driver's seat.

Phil and I grinned as Dad started the car and swung it around and out of the parking lot. He crowed on for the entire ride home as Mom interjected her thoughts on what had transpired. Dad explained what the other guys said and how they razzed him for hours. He screamed about how we might have been dead along the highway somewhere for all he knew. Then Dad went on about silly superstitions taking over Mom's little mind. He realized something as drastic as moving Mom to a rest home was essential. Controversial? Surely. Exciting for Phil and me? You bet!

Dad's anguish over freeing Mom from bondage increased when she didn't get better, despite Doctor Simmon's medication and prayers. He moved Mom into a place called Ridgecliff Hospital, a mental facility that sat on an imposing hill in Euclid. It quite possibly held off armies based on geography. It looked like people entered but never came out. After Mom settled in as a *guest*, Shirley readied us for a visit, and we were eager to see Mom, but not that hospital.

For youngsters, the three-story brick building sitting on a long, winding driveway intimidated me. Maybe we'd heard too many horror flicks, but we went inside. I stayed close to Shirley as we parked. Our eyes moved side to side as we got into a waiting area. Shirley got us signed in, and we waited. The place looked like a jail. It left an indelible impression on us all.

We waited a few minutes before Dad came bounding up to get us. He waved his hand, and we followed him to Mom's small, plain hospital room. Long curtains almost covered the windows, allowing a small stream of light to enter. Mom sat up on the bed, dressed in a blue hospital gown. She smiled and held out her arms for a hug. Phil and I obliged and asked many questions in a machine-gun style. We asked when she'd come home.

"Well, soon, I suppose, Mom answered, it all depends on what Doctor Simmons recommends."

Mom was surprisingly rational. She displayed a faraway look in her eyes, but didn't seem doped up on medications. We conversed briefly, and Dad suggested we go outside because the place gave everyone the creeps anyway. Nobody would've blinked if Boris Karloff poked his head from behind a curtain. Ridgecliff scared the holy fire right out of us.

Dad led us to the guard shack and warned us about how far we went into the courtyard. We headed straight for a shaded area of picnic tables. I thought it ironic about a picnic on the grounds of a sanitarium, but I sat beside Mom.

Phil and I were bored with the talk of how this person or that one resided there for years. We wandered away, always under the watchful eye of adults. A man walked towards us, and I tensed up. Phil headed back for safety.

"Hey, kid, can I tell you about my dream?" The strange man asked me in a nervous, slurred speech.

I wondered what to do next. I ran for it and trotted twenty yards back to where I was. The man kept pace!

"Hey, the man yelled, hey, I gotta tell you about my dream! I...I..., gotta tell you!"

Dad's eyes squinted like John Wayne's just before he released a volley of hot lead. He stood up and put his arms out in a locked manner to slow the loony storyteller. He stepped into the man's pathway—Dad's turn to talk.

"Hey, buddy, my son doesn't want to hear your story, okay? Move along, and everything will be fine." Dad insisted.

The man stammered about some dream, but Dad decided we'd seen enough.

"Look, pal, we won't want your story. Take off, or I'll get the guards!" Dad said.

The guy got the hint, and I moved back behind Mom and Shirley. He may have been harmless, but we were taking no chances.

Days went by after we left there. Poor Dad felt as if he had abandoned Mom and didn't rest well. He saw her as often as necessary and kept in constant contact with Doctor Simmons. Phil and I heckled Dad about Mom coming home. My grandparents, too, kept the heat on him. Mamaw believed she'd done nothing to affect Mom's mental state and theorized that Mom had been seeking attention. Nobody pulled stunts like Mom to be normal. She was ill but not sick enough for the place where she was trapped. Dad came up with a plan to do something.

Doctor Simmons gave Dad his two-week evaluation. Mom was depressed and needed shock treatments to bring her to a helpful state of mind. Dad's fury rose when asked about Mom's release. The good doctor said he'd test her with shock therapy before releasing her. Dad begged to differ on the treatment plan.

Dad whisked Phil and me into the car and headed for the hospital. He told us little, except to stay in the car when he went inside. He told us to keep our mouths shut.

Dad parked behind the building. To our surprise, Linda parked her car beside us. She smiled and waved, putting her fingers in front of her mouth to keep us from speaking. We got the hint and sat there quietly. A Stefanow storm brewed, and it felt like "Mission Impossible" to me. Sheer fun!

We waited in the car, bored out of our ever-loving minds. We dared not make a peep. We went to a "rest" home. I wanted the whole mess over and for Mom to be well again.

Some commotion occurred inside the building! Muscular orderlies moved the people outside. Whatever developed involved dear old Dad. Phil and I waited in anticipation.

Dad ran out a side door, pulling Mom quickly. Struggling to keep up, she moved like a cartoon character. We laughed as Dad shoved Mom into our car, her blue gown flapping in the breeze. Dad popped the keys into the car's ignition, dropped the gearshift into reverse, and made our big Mercury use all eight cylinders.

Dad didn't like to make a habit of passing up red lights and stop signs, but on our wild ride home, he did just that. We were temporary fugitives. We heard of Bonnie and Clyde, but "Gus and Em" had yet to be written.

We spent the next day getting phone calls from Dr. Simmons. (The Eastlake Police came by, and Dad admitted his actions. No harm, no foul!) Dad didn't want Mom to be used for shock treatments that threatened her shaken psyche. Mom's return helped us get our lives back. Did it work? Only time would reveal what normal might be in our house.

CHAPTER TEN

As if things weren't kooky enough for this Stefanow clan, Dad needed back surgery number three for scar tissue removal. He put it off because his Plant Manager job kept many souls under his command. In a salaried position, Dad worked many eighty-hour weeks. Phil and I took great joy when he came home, but one particular day, we did *not*.

Mom lived as an acute disciplinarian. Her judge-jury-executioner style meant getting away with *nothing*. She practiced no "wait 'til your father gets home" scare tactics. The punishment came "right now" and violently. Mom brought us into the world and vowed to take us back out if necessary. Push her buttons-pay the price. Everybody understood it.

Phil and I got rowdy with Mom on the phone. No one ever knew why. She'd grit her teeth, give a classic "Uh...uh!" or stare a hole through us. This day, she tried something new after multiple painful attempts at corralling her two "jackals." When Dad got home, she made her wishes known.

"Gus beat the boys and beat them good, too! I've beat them 'til I am blue in the face! Why those two heathens caught me on the phone with that neighbor who talks too much! You gotta do somethin'!" Mom demanded.

"Jesus, Mary, and Joseph, Emily, can I get both feet in the door? I worked twelve hours on concrete and ain't even taken my shoes off yet! And you, a grown woman who loves knockin' them around, can't control two kids?" Dad shot back.

Mom told him we were waiting on death row, AKA my bedroom upstairs. Dad couldn't be the beating kind, so we were confident we'd work something out.

"You two! You two! What makes you so ignorant? You know your mom can't wait to set your butts on fire, and you provoke her! I'm raisin' dummies doin' their *spite work*!" Dad bellowed.

We assumed the position at the end of the bed and leaned over with our butts in the air. Dad removed his belt, an eerie sound as the pant loops slowed his momentum. He drew back the belt, and with a "wham", he hit the footboard!

He drew back again and repeated the sequence. Phil and I stood up, astonished yet relieved. Dad leaned over and whispered this:

"Make on dummies like I am killing you! Wait five minutes, rub your eyes well, wet your face, and mess up your hair before coming downstairs!"

Dad continued beating the footboard as we hooted it up nicely! "Oh, you're killing me," and "No, daddy, no" seemed like Oscar-worthy statements. He glared as if to say, "Don't overdo it."

We went downstairs, and Mom gave her favorite "I told you so" speech about how much harder Dad hit. Dad showered and took his place in his easy chair. The man could have slept in a spewing volcano anytime at our house.

A few nights later, with Dad still late at work, Mom called Phil, me, and Papaw to the table. The spread consisted of Vienna sausages, tomato sauce, saltine crackers, and green beans. Mom was a Southern soul to the core.

Papaw sipped his customary Stroh's beer in his favorite tumbler while the rest had Kool-Aid. Mom dished the feast, and Papaw talked up his job progress.

Felipe (Phil) looked quizzical and disgusted as Mom doled out dinner. I looked at him beside me and shot him a "What's up, Doc?" smirk. He leaned over and caught me off guard, whispering but getting louder each time.

"Gus, monkey peckers, monkey *peckers*!"

If anyone could break up a given day, it was my little brother. I tried biting my lip, putting my head down, and turning away from Mom, holding in a laugh that suffocated me!

Mom got a whiff of what was going on and promptly began the interrogation! There was no way she'd let anything slip past her.

"Phillip, what is your problem, young man? Get to eatin' and eatin' right now, you understand?" Mom said forcefully.

I tried to give Phil the do-not-answer glare, but he plodded on in his quest for comedic immortality. His *life* was on the line.

"Mommy. Uh, I can't eat those things! Why I saw in school the Geographic magazine, and well, these sausages look like, uh, monkey peckers!"

My poor grandfather choked on his cold beer and coughed loudly, violently spraying his plate! Mom sat in disbelief, unable to process what she had just heard. Her wheels spun inside her head.

"Why, my Lord, Phillip, my God, how do you think of these things? Why you, you ain't right, you little monster! I cannot believe what I'm a-hearin' in my own house!"

I held out as long as possible before spewing laughter like an effervescent stomach medicine or Old Faithful. I was G-O-N-E, gone!

"And you, Junior, the big brother, just another hyena a-settin' in my house! You keep him makin' these stupid cracks with your big laughin', well, mister, neither of you will be laughin' when your dad gets home! I can't believe the heathens I am raisin'! I'm sorry, Dad, about these two idiots!" Mom railed on.

Papaw looked over his glasses and shook his head. He rarely said more than a few words at a time. He grunted and began his response.

"Junior, I understand your Mamaw a-callin' you tetched, but Phillip, you done passed whatever that is! You plumb-crazy, buddy! You won't be long in this world with your actions, little man! Monkey peckers, Great God a-mighty! Always actin' a-fool!"

Now, it was Round Two in the outrageous belly laughter in the kitchen. Mom, for her part, disgustedly took her meal into the living room to keep from murdering us right there. Papaw cleaned up his mess and went for another beer while Mom pledged to take over Dad's dinner duties the next time. I made a meal out of the beans and crackers.

As stated, Mom hadn't planned dinner the following evening, so she asked Dad to make something. He protested, mentioned something about being "Hop-Sing" from Bonanza, and found canned beef stew in the cupboard. Hooray. Papaw was spared only by a quick trip to the Bluegrass State for a long weekend.

Dad cussed under his breath, awake but grumpy as he prepared our meal. Tornado, our one-hundred-pound Collie-Shepherd mix dog, awaited his evening meal, too.

With everything ready, Dad called us to the table. He went to the can opener and retrieved the dog's meal. He set the dish down, and Tornado almost ate the bowl too.

Mom came over last as Dad put four bowls down. Something about the smell of the food hit us hard. I looked into my bowl and saw a biscuit and something that looked like black licorice or an animal vein! Mom went on about her long phone calls, not looking at her meal. When she looked down, she quickly looked back up! Mom bolted from the table, and the "Eck, eck, eck" vomitus warning sign went out. She stuffed a napkin into her mouth and wouldn't come back. Tissues were her preference, but she used hankies or scarves in a pinch!

Dad plunked a fork into his "stew" and tried cutting a hunk of meat. Phil, with an upturned nose, spoke up.

"Daddy, uh, Dad, that stuff isn't right! Oh my God, *you gave us the dog food*! Hahahaha! Jesus, Tornado got our stew! Gus, this is great! Hahaha! There goes Mom, Eck, eck, eck, eck! Hahaha!" Phil rejoiced.

"Oh, you're crazy! Maybe this ain't the best beef stew, but come on!" Dad protested.

Upon further review, Dad agreed with us. He went upstairs to apologize to Mom, and I had to dump the evidence in the dogs' bowl. Our family went out for dinner that night, whether we liked it or not.

Something happened each year that made our vacations memorable. So, with Mom's illness in full swing, Dad insisted we vacation in Pennsylvania and New Jersey. We brought an ample supply of Mom's medication.

Phil and I were little punks with Mom and her easily upset stomach. We took turns pointing out the nature that breathed last on the roads. Phil relished attracting Mom's attention to the ample roadkill we'd see on long trips.

"Mommy, did you see that dead skunk on the highway? Man, he looked like some of Mamaw's marmalade came out of his mouth! Yuck! It's everywhere!" Phil boasted.

Mom missed *one* dead carcass, but my little Felipe would not let it happen. Dad ground his teeth and cussed about how we ignorant boys took pleasure in Mom's misery. Mom clasped a tissue over her mouth and began the "Eck...eck" sound again!

Mom begged Dad to pull over in heavy traffic so she could vomit. I laughed too hard to notice her open hand swing over the backseat in Phil's direction. Phil cackled, "A swing and a miss!" as Mom whiffed, unusual for her. She often didn't even look at us, whacking both boys with her jewelry-clad fingers.

Dad pulled over, and Mom leaped out, running up a hill and puking—lecture time from Daddy, dearest.

"Jesus, Christopher, Phillip! You gotta find every dead animal? I got two spiteful morons! Ain't your mother got enough troubles? Miserable kids!"

Mom recovered and threatened Phil and me with instant death IF we pointed out any more mangled animals. A momentary truce went into place.

We loved seeing Dad's relations since it seemed like Kentucky came around too often. We left Pennsylvania and headed towards rich Uncle Phil's place in New Jersey.

We came to a stop sign, and Dad asked which direction Jersey was. I peered over my baseball cards and told him to take a right. He should have checked himself.

We drove for an hour and a half. I dozed off but was startled by Dad cussing about Maryland license plates. He pulled onto the first exit. I would rather have been sleeping.

Dad stopped at a service station, and we sat there like ignorant tourists. Phil laughed about my messed-up hair, and Dad came back looking for yours truly.

"Gusty, when I asked about that sign ninety miles ago, what did you tell me?" Dad inquired.

"Well, it said right. I thought..." I said before Dad interrupted.

"Yeah, you were so positive that we are now in Maryland! Dad yelled, " We've driven the wrong way! I'll never ask you again about reading a road sign! Jesus, Mary, and Joseph!"

Phil got a hefty charge out of Dad yelling, but why listen to a kid for directions? Mom defended me, and everyone shouted about being stuck in another state. I rationalized my mistake with Dad by reminding him about going off the beaten path for caves, Indian villages, or other tourist traps. My plea didn't work. Dad fueled the car, and we sped off!

We wound down crowded streets and passed a massive Catholic Church, Saint Somebody's. Mom got that familiar faraway look on her face. She shouted at Dad, causing him to let go of the wheel.

"Gus, pass that church one more time!" She screeched.

Dad went through this drill before. Mom did it when passing churches, funeral homes, and cemeteries. Phil and I had the job of distracting her when we passed them, but we missed some. Mom needed to pass it again to keep from dying, or so she believed. Dad cussed, and we headed past our friends at the fuel station.

"Emily, is that good enough?" Dad asked.

Mom sat there and blurted out, "No, pass it again!" Dad burned as he sped over the posted speed limit. We looked pretty stupid, but we were getting *used* to it!

Dad drove us around the block. This time, Phil got an evil grin and decided to have fun. He did it as his way of dealing with Mom. He wanted laughs!

As we passed the service station, Phil waved like a madman at the attendants. They stared in wonderment and half-waved back. Phil howled with laughter, and I smiled, covering my face to keep my parents from hearing me. We laughed to keep from crying.

The routine went on for three more passes before Dad came unglued. He accommodated Mom and her ways. While everyone else analyzed her, Dad gave in with deep love. The scene proved too much, though, as Dad appeared to have smoke billowing out of his ears.

"Emily, holy Christopher, you see people coming out to see the idiot family from Ohio", Dad barked, " We'll be lucky if they don't call the cops! Can we please go to my brother's house? Ridiculous!"

"Gus, I can't! Something terrible will happen, I know it! I will die if we don't make these trips, and I can't go on!" Mom shouted back.

"Oh, you're right. Something terrible will happen, Dad said, as he pounded his fist on the dashboard. I may go out of my mind, too. You want that? A man can only stand so much!" He yelled back as he drove.

A crowd gathered, and Phil waved, laughing like a clown, as we poked by. I shrank in my seat, laughing, keeping anyone from seeing me. Phil ate up his celebrity status. Dad caught a glimpse of his "fun" and reminded us that Mom's sickness was legitimate.

"Oh, you think this is some joke, eh? Do you? Your mother's a sick person, and you want to make fun? Ignorant, miserable kids!" Dad howled. We were in trouble again.

We couldn't laugh our way out of the situation. We apologized, saying we were waving to the friendly locals. Dad waved to strangers in Kentucky, even pulling up and talking with them, but didn't buy the bull we were selling in Maryland. Our butts were on trial!

Mom snapped from her stupor, and we entered the interstate towards Pennsylvania. We headed to see Uncle Phil's family, knowing he would make things right. He and Dad would shoot pool, cuss at each other for cheating, and relive the good ol' days. Life didn't get any better.

We had a ball with our favorite uncle. He took us to batting cages and amusement parks. He let us play with his elaborate train set, the size of Texas, in his basement. Visiting Uncle Phil in Jersey made our suffering worthwhile. The return home proved uneventful. Hallelujah!

Dad's third back surgery ended his working days. Things changed at home with him around full-time, but he got involved in the Fraternal Order of Police, we'll always believe, to avoid tickets. He played cards with the cops every month! Dad also spent a lot of time at Eastlake Little League because he epitomized a Type A personality. He'd find some way to fidget on a bed of nails!

Mom began "normalcy" with Little League baseball. She got involved with the women's auxiliary by working the concession stand and doing the annual program books. Her outreach beyond herself meant a great deal to everyone. The emphasis on self and others transformed her in ways nothing else did. She blossomed in her new role.

Civic duties came naturally for Mom and Dad. Both became presidents of the Little League and the Ladies Auxiliary and held the positions for decades. Both were known for being selfless givers to those in need. Mom gave away toys Phil and I enjoyed, many of which are now in museums. She gave items to neighbors before selling them at garage sales. Those same sales netted us instant cash for our visit to Kentucky.

Papaw's five years with us were rewarding, but when he retired in 1976 and moved to Kentucky, he gave up on life. His black lung from years in the mines and the smoking habit took their toll on him.

City kids like Phil and me bored quickly at Mamaw and Papaw's, but things were not dull for long with Dad there. Sitting on a hot porch at night gave Dad time to stir the pot, ending all peace.

"Hey Willie (Papaw's actual name), remember that Kit-Kat Club in Akron? Man, the fun there. Those honky-tonks were for ladies, men like us! How's that song you like go? 'If you've got the money, honey, I got the time...somethin' like that, huh?" Dad crowed.

Mamaw leaned forward in her rocking chair, squinting and aiming accusatory eyes at my unfortunate grandfather. The fire stoked under Mamaw's chair got her ire way up.

"Yeah, what about it, Willie? Up there in Ohio, doing what you ain't supposed to? A-skirt chasin' just like I always thought! Ho-in' round, Willie! I set here a-raisin' these young-uns, and you're off a-chasin' nasty women! Why on top of the earth, do I suffer like I do?" Mamaw said tersely.

"Gus, why, oh why, do you hate my guts? Why there ain't a word of truth in that! And you know what's worse? That woman is going to ride me after you all go home! She won't quit-she does! Stupid, stupid forner!" Papaw complained in the *longest* speech he ever gave.

Dad tickled himself so much that he held his side, and his eyes watered! His joy was complete, and he chuckled as Mamaw went inside, cussing Papaw as she went.

Poor Papaw repeated his pleas for Dad to quit. Mom jumped on Dad for interfering in her parents' business and causing trouble. Once Dad got tickled about anything, it took him time to cool down. Dad took very little in life too seriously. Mom told Mamaw the truth, but a little too late. Papaw's gallows awaited!

Our return trip went fine until Dad passed a cop in the right lane of the highway, doing the posted, idiotic 55-mph speed limit. Dad crept up beside the guy as Mom slept. Dad did the next best thing when the officer didn't speed up.

We passed the cop, and Dad barely got the car in the lane before the lights and siren went on. Phil and I remembered Dad's FOPA connections. The test of wills began! The cop came to our car, shaking his head.

Dad pulled out his license and police auxiliary card. The cop looked very unimpressed.

"Buddy, that card grants no impunity to speeding! I mean, you just drove right by me? How dumb can you get?" The cop inquired.

"Look, you were blocking the traffic flow by loafing! If everyone went fifty-five, nobody would get anywhere!" Dad said.

Mom woke up and started talking about tickets costing money. Dad waved her off with an "Eh, eh!" flick of his hand. He did that when he wanted silence. Fat chance!

The cop gave Dad a warning ticket and hoped he'd slow him down. "Yeah, Dad said, by about ten minutes!" Home sweet homecoming.

We weren't home long before we hit the road again. Papaw went to the hospital with a heart attack. His health went downhill. Mom fed him his last meal before she and Mamaw went home to clean up. Dad, Tim, and I stayed with him until his heart rate dropped to twenty-five beats per minute. Dad ordered us away, and Papaw had passed by the time we visited the break room down the hall. Dad would not let us see him die.

The rock of Mom's clan breathed its last. His promise to take me raccoon hunting, as he called it, never came. Funeral prep took center stage. We all missed Papaw's quiet strength.

Back in the day, everyone paid respects at the funeral home. Cousin Ralph showed up in a Buick wagon. Phil and I approached, but we shouldn't have.

"Hey, boy, you want some Kentucky border baloney sammidges?" Ralph inquired.

Inside his car were several coolers filled with food. He wore a white t-shirt covered in mustard, mayo, and God only knows what else. Our appetites vanished.

Also inside his car were his oldest son, Donnie, and the ugliest Chihuahua dog, a rodent named "Chaboogie," an instant classic. Our faces gave up what we were thinking.

"Boy, I got the best food you all could ask for in here! Don't be bashful!" Ralph begged.

Little Chaboogie ran up and over Ralph, onto the dashboard, and then onto the coolers. Ralph called him everything but a hound dog while striving to catch the tiny troublemaker.

"Chaboogie, Chaboogie, get over here, you monster. Them fellers want to get a bite to eat, and you're ruinin' it for them!" Ralph screamed as Donnie tried catching the dog, too. The scene with two rotund men flopping around after a nasty little dog couldn't have been funnier, and nobody could make it up.

Phil and I saw, heard, and *smelled* enough. Uncle Dick's barn seemed cleaner than Ralph's Buick. Back inside the House-Rawlings Funeral home, we went.

Mom's state of mind prevented her from attending her father's funeral. She stayed at Mamaw's house while Dad represented us with the required "nobody-leaves-the-body-unattended" contingency inside the funeral home. Leave it to Dad to get into trouble.

Crazy cousin Frank and Dad were pals, or criminal partners, for years. Frank was a part of Uncle Dick's clan. He called Dad "Hunky," and Dad called him "Hillbilly," but neither cared.

The other mourners left at dusk. Dad and Frank took turns daring each other to open unauthorized doors like a couple of teenage explorers.

Frank found an unlocked door and went in, crossing a line for Dad to mimic. Frank wandered around with the lights out before exiting.

"Hunky, we're playin' a game, but don't go in that dark room. It'll fosho scare you back to Cleveland!" Frank uttered.

Challenge accepted for Dad. He wasn't letting his pal one-up him ever!

Dad crept into the room while Frank stood guard and ensured "lights out" was applied. Dad rummaged around, walking into exam tables and glass cabinets. Frank hadn't warned him about the odor in the room. Something smelled burnt.

Dad found a mobile clothes rack with plastic bags hanging from it. Feeling his way around, he felt something like crispy bacon and yanked his hand back hard. Out of the room, he went, not caring how much Frank laughed at him.

Both men went back to Papaw's casket for the remaining vigil. Frank told returning mourners the next day about the escapades.

"Yeah, and Hunky over here got the bejesus scared outta him when he touched somethin' in that dark room," Frank said over snickers and howls.

Several mourners looked at the two idiots incredulously. Hadn't they heard about the tanker truck explosion on the highway that night? Didn't they know two people got burned beyond recognition in the wreck?

Dad and Frank looked very sickly at one another, neither man speaking. Pranks at the funeral home ended. Both men grew up a little, and the clowning halted. Papaw was gone but never forgotten as we headed into the 1980s.

CHAPTER ELEVEN

The Stefanow family's love for the holidays started with my parents, and Christmas was the biggest deal. Sure, we celebrated the others like good Americans, but the charm of Christmas mesmerized us. Both folks were more loving and in better moods for the annual event. Phil and I were on our best behavior from Halloween until December 26th, hoping our parents kept short accounts for the rest of the year.

Dad missed Mom and Pop Stefanow most during the season and may have overcompensated for the loss by overdoing the stretched budget thing each year. Christmas brought out his inner child for a man able to restrain himself fiscally. One of Dad's enduring qualities, immaturity, is what is most loved about him. If the public didn't like a silly man, so be it. Pretty happy being himself, he believed nothing accentuated it more than Christmas. With trays of nuts and hard candies lying about, the Christmas music capped off a loving, tender time of year.

Mom, long before anyone heard of a love language, loved gifts. She didn't *care* what time of year she received them. Giving and receiving gifts were just what a person did as naturally as breathing or eating. In her mind, this may have been her private circle of life. One bought an item, then sold it as excess inventory or gave it away to make room to buy more. Mom wore the coveted badge of "consumer" like the God-blessed, flag-waving patriot she portrayed herself as!

Living through the Great Depression affected how parents responded to poverty and want. Neither allowed anyone to go hungry, ever. Both were generous, even to a fault. The grand Christmas celebration started well before the neighbor's decor! If there were such a thing as a family *living* Christmas, we tried. The season of giving was perpetual and intentional.

We lived on Naumann Avenue in Euclid, Ohio, for years. I was four years old when I noticed how different our household felt near Christmas. It seemed a kinder, gentler time for all of us. Dad whistled a carol or two (The Little Drummer Boy, his personal favorite) and displayed joy. Even during her most challenging times, Mom never let them interfere with our celebrations.

One Christmas Eve in Euclid, I stood on our landing between staircases in the giant house. I heard the rustle of wrapping paper, scissors cutting something, and general "Oh, they're gonna like this" comments from my sisters and parents. I wanted to check my presents out before morning. A creaky step announced my presence, and I got busted!

Dad put me back in bed and promised Santa would come by only if I slept. Huh, why were they the ones wrapping stuff, then? I stayed in bed and stared at the ceiling.

About ten minutes later, as I lay there wide awake, I heard a magical sound on the roof! It...sounded like footsteps! One, then another, and then "HO-HO-HO, MERRY CHRISTMAS," I heard in our chimney. Holy mackerel, I needed sleep right away! I covered my head under the blankets and hid from the man himself!

The night's activities made me firmly believe in Santa for at least another decade. Years later, Dad admitted that he paid a dumb boyfriend of my sister to climb a two-story house covered in ice and snow to make me a believer! It's worth noting that the lad lived through the danger.

In the 1970s, the world experienced global cooling, with longer, colder, and snowier winters expected. We prepared for another Ice Age with fossil fuels running out. Our schools' old boiler heating systems didn't keep up, and we spent weeks at home with a mountain of assignments to hand in once school reopened. The President begged us to dress comfortably but keep the thermostats set to a cooler temperature so everyone could make it through winter.

After his working years ended, Dad wanted to find Mom a practical gift that would help with our national crisis. He took Phil and me to Kmart to get Mom something warm for Christmas. We were so proud of ourselves. Nobody could beat *thinking* Stefanow's!

We found a long, thick velour robe with a belt that seemed perfect. Mom needed warmth on the darkest, coldest days of a Cleveland winter. We congratulated ourselves profusely and got the gift home. We helped Dad wrap it and stick it under the Christmas tree. Mom's reaction would be priceless.

Christmas morning, Phil and I leaped from bed with our usual vigor. Financially, our family experienced a three-year dry spell while Dad awaited a decision from Social Security. The mountain of gifts was scaled back, but we celebrated regardless.

We gathered in our living room, and Dad turned on the stereo, playing Harry Simeon Chorale's Little Drummer Boy album. The all-out assault began!

Phil and I tore into our gifts like bears in a honey pot! Paper flew like confetti in a parade. We'd open a gift, examine it for ten seconds, and then grab the next one like a fantasy assembly line! We realized Mom opened nothing while taking pictures with the Polaroid camera. Oh no, she needed the robe!

Dad called for a timeout in action. He passed our wrapped robe to give to Mom. She didn't want to halt our momentum, but we insisted!

Mom opened the gift and unfolded our prize. The color seemed perfect, so she stood up and looked at our wall of mirrors near the love beads that separated the dining and living areas. (This is a 1970s must-have in any home.) She made quick poses with the robe. Her face looked like she'd seen a specter as she turned toward us. Her lips curled downward, tears formed in her eyes, and she tossed the robe at Dad!

Mom sprinted across the Christmas carnage like an Olympian, dodging packages and furniture. She moaned about a "horse blanket" as she rocketed upstairs.

The look on Dad's face showed him going from anger to disbelief and back again. He stood up and negotiated the disastrous Christmas offerings on the floor! He stood at the base of the stairs, pleading his case.

"Hey, Emily! What is it? Come on, now, it's Christmas! What's wrong? Holy Christopher, you try, and you try! I give up!" Dad exclaimed.

Phil and I looked at each other. What do we do now? Mom's off on a fit, and we had presents to open! The celebration must go on! Dad's guidance came swiftly.

"Boys, go ahead! I don't know what we did wrong this year! We'll find out when your mom calms down."

Phil and I were happier than woodpeckers in a lumber yard! We dove into toys, clothes, and albums. Eventually, Mom appeared and explained herself.

"I...I just saw a horse blanket, kids! I mean, the only thing missin' is Clint Eastwood! That robe belongs on a mule, and I ain't no mule. I'm as sorry as I can be; I won't wear that! I look as big as a house in it!" Mom insisted as mist covered her bloodshot eyes.

Dad opened gifts from Mom. Dad's love language, acts of service, meant that giving and getting gifts delighted him, too. Mom made Dad a well-dressed Stefanow man all his days. Although he might not have a nickel to his name, well, by God, he wouldn't look like it! Image meant everything in our home. If we couldn't dazzle folks with nonsense, we'd overwhelm them with pomp and circumstance.

The following day, in a fate worse than death, Dad and I returned the robe to Kmart. Back then, Kmart would've taken cow manure back and given shoppers something for it! We took cold, hard cash and an important lesson. Dad never tried guessing what to buy again. He took Mom out, got what she wanted, wrapped it, and put it under the tree. He'd tell Mom, "Act like you're surprised come Christmas morning, okay, Emily?"

Our poverty lasted several years before Dad's settlement with Social Security. We got what Mom called "Hillbilly-rich" for a while, having no limits on birthdays and Christmas celebrations. Our near-middle-class status even embarrassed us at times.

On a cold, snowy night, a week before Christmas 1979, Bing Crosby blasted out on our brand-new HIFI stereo/faux-fireplace combo. Colorfully wrapped packages sat atop our new couch and loveseat, towering five feet high. The new carpeting showed an American family living the dream. From the outside, things seemed perfect.

I changed Bing's album for Nat King Cole and saw strange lights on our street. I ran to the peephole and looked out to see a Santa Claus, several elves, and multiple City of Eastlake trucks in our driveway.

Mom, busy cleaning the oven, arms covered in rubber gloves, scraped away the annual residue. I required smarts when breaking the news!

"Mom, there's someone at the door you're going to want to see!" I said with excitement in my teenage voice.

"Who is it, Junior? I ain't got no time for visitors with my arms up in this here oven! Who is it?" Mom inquired.

Phil and I both ducked and spoke when answering Mom. The belt or backyard switches (Translation- sticks) had less effect on teenagers than a well-timed right hook! Approaching the wrong way was likened to putting one's hand in a garbage disposal and praying it did not come on!

"Uh, well, it's uh, *Santa Claus*!" I roared. "Jesus, Mary, and Joseph, when I want a joke, I'll make one myself!" Mom replied as she pulled back a fist. Her reddish-brown hair stood on end like Larry Fine of Three Stooges fame or Heat-Miser from "The Year without a Santa Claus."

I recoiled and managed a "No, I am not kidding" line as I stepped away from the fist.

"Lord, have mercy! Oh, go and answer that door. If you tell anyone I am home, I will kill you!" Mom commanded.

Phil flew up the stairs, scouting from the second-story window while my sentry duties kicked in. Santa seemed a pleasant fellow and delivered a great Christmas for those "in need' this year! Oh boy! Poor Santa stood in shock.

Santa entered our living room and took a long look around. He muttered about us "having it tough this year," but his voice trailed off as he took everything in stride. We didn't stash our goodies! The man shook his head, and the elves carried three large boxes of food, toys with broken games, and a giant turkey. I ushered them out the door while Mom was silent on our basement steps. Whew! We got by, but Mom's fury spiked!

"Who could've done this? Who? Your Dad is off with them cops a-playin' cards while I'm here embarrassed out of my mind! Someone turned us in to the city! I know that darn Santa, too! I think he's Irwin or Irving or somethin' like that! Oh, Lord! The whole street knows now, too! I'm going to kill someone!" Mom promised.

I reminded her of the season of goodwill, but it went nowhere. Embarrassing my folks came with a steep price. We have yet to discover who revealed our need during the blessed Christmas season. Some *spite work* from a mischievous soul at the holidays went down like last year's fruitcake.

Dad loved Christmas best, but Thanksgiving showed off his culinary skills. He prepped a meal each year to mark the Noon NFL kickoff. People set their watches to it, no lie!

Mom prepared the "fixins," as she called them, but Dad got the bird. He scoped one out at the local Pic-n-Pay store like the Hope diamond! The turkey needed to weigh x number of pounds, be a specific shape for the roasting pan, and be on sale. Dad also made the stuffing by supplementing a box variety with his additional requirements. Nobody asked what those were.

Dad arose at dawn each year to see his bird perfection for the masses. Mom rose later to set up the relish tray and make pumpkin pies, mashed potatoes, etc. The rest of us made ourselves scarce during the cooking or faced extinction. If there was one day of the year on which my folks were guaranteed conflict, Thanksgiving of all days provided tug-of-war fireworks!

My parents' kitchen reflected no Julia Child soundstage. This production facility needed work done. Sure, there were outbursts of "Gusty, one more time you move my salt and I swear I'll salt you and put your big Stefanow butt in this oven!" Dad's reply? "Look, shake a leg, we got a lot of people comin' here, Emily! Let's move!"

The cacophony of activity continued each year. Dad, ever the production supervisor, was on pins and needles about the meal being ready. Feeling that perfection came slow and steady, Mom did not cotton to Dad's assumed leadership in her kitchen. The proximity of sharp instruments added suspense.

One year at Thanksgiving, Parson and Hettie came by for dessert. They liked our new stereo/fireplace/catchall in the living room. Parson tried warming his hands on it.

"Gettin' some heat, Parson, are you?" Dad inquired.

"Yeah, sure, this thing is nice, Gusty! I gotta get me one of these too!" Parson remarked.

Dad, always the king of sarcasm and pranks, told Parson to get a little closer, and he'd turn the heat up. Dad opened the top of the stereo and pretended to adjust the spinning, orange light bulb in the fake fireplace. Each time he turned the knob, the stereo got louder and louder.

Parson stepped back quizzically while the wives went off into another room. Phil and I hurried away so as not to give away the joke.

"Go ahead, Parson, I'll crank that heat!" Dad bellowed. To hide his smile, he turned away. As soon as Parson got close, Dad blasted the stereo volume through the roof and made the preacher jump like LeBron James! The joke ended, but Parson shook his head in disbelief.

Dad held his side and laughed as his inner child possessed him. Parson made a keen observation.

"Man, you get me to come all the way out here to do that? That ain't right, and you know it! I can take a joke like anyone, but you actin' a fool on

Thanksgivin' shows your *reprobate* mind! And I'd hate to see what you'd do if you didn't like me!" Parson said.

Mom and Hettie did not even break from their conversation about the kids. They saw enough of this behavior through the years that it didn't faze them. Then it was on to coffee and pumpkin pie for the whole gang.

Although Dad got free rein for turkeys each year, Mom held back everything else. The man's fascination with pumpkin pie stemmed from his father's homemade pies that no one could duplicate. Dad tried altering Mom's recipe, and it only produced problems. Colorful language permeated the kitchen, with thanks having nothing to do with it. Regardless, Dad doled out cuts of pie for everyone.

Because our meal centered on an early start, Dad had already consumed more than his share of the pie, as Mom kept him on the "straight and narrow" with the inventory. An evening of thanks became an impromptu contest between Parson and Dad for pie supremacy. Gluttony received a Baptist indulgence, approved by followers everywhere. Praise the Lord and pass the calories.

Mom glanced at Dad with each pie piece he put down. Hettie warned Parson about his sugar level, and he quit. Dad marched on while Mom warned him.

"Gusty, I bet you've eaten a whole pie today alone! You get sick, and I'm going to laugh at your stupidity! Hettie, you can't tell a man nothin', I swear!"

Hettie approved of every word. She and Parson gave out hugs and never left without an "I love you" at any get-together. They went home, but the fun began later.

The house's silence was broken at about 1 in the morning. The shuffling of Dad's feet on the carpet and the way he always bumped into something woke me up. Dad couldn't creep if he tried, be it a lamp, chair, or innumerable obstacles. His illness gave Mom a bizarre moment of rejoicing. No kidding.

"See, stupid, I told you! You love your pies, sure. How do they taste right about now? Stupid, stupid man!" Mom said.

Dad returned to bed, albeit a little lighter than when he'd left. How much pie had he downed? Nobody knew, but there'd be a tipping point or recompense to satisfy. Fully awake, I shrewdly removed my tape recorder from under my bed, as any teenage son would. It would be ammunition for later days.

About fifteen minutes later, "Gus the Geyser" returned to the bathroom. Phil was also awake, and I sprang into action. I got the recorder near the bathroom door for the pie expulsion. What valuable blackmail material!

I returned to our bedroom, and Phil buried his head into his pillow. Hilarity always broke out at our house when the other guy got sick!

Mom went on about the warning that Dad didn't heed. I told Phil that this transgression beat Dad's fiftieth birthday boondoggle. He drank a full fifth of Seagram's Seven, his favorite spirit, and I kept that on tape for a long time until Dad threatened to break my machine. I kept my new recording hidden.

Dehydration, a real threat, caused Dad to seek out something he'd keep in his stomach. Mom offered to go downstairs for water, but Dad would not hear it. Sick, he went into his well-known trot down the stairs. There, he met Phil's belt on the staircase.

Our family's laziness about climbing upstairs meant we stuffed anything we planned to take up later there, with good intentions. It only sometimes worked out. So, Dad trotted down and dumped his body weight on the belt prong. Shazam!

"Oh, Emily, help me! I swear, these stupid kids! My foot, oh Jesus, my foot!" Dad cried.

Mom, unmoved like the Rock of Gibraltar, had been the object of decades of routine pranks and jokes. She sat up in bed and bellowed back.

"Gus, I am not comin' down the stairs! Have you done enough fer one night? Lord, have mercy!"

"Hey, Emily, I ain't playin' this time! Oh, this stupid belt! Oh, my foot! Come help me, holy Toledo, this hurts!" Dad begged.

Mom protested, grabbed a robe, and bounded down the hallway as Phil and I scrambled to look on. The argument would be priceless if Dad tricked her again!

Dad, a grown man, stood at the bottom of our steps with a kid's belt stuck to his foot! Sure enough, about two inches of steel prong were embedded in his heel.

"Well, dummy, pull the belt out! Mom roared, "You gotta get that thing out of there! You don't want me to pull it!"

Dad took a deep breath, reached down, and gave it a yank! Wow, did he let out a yell? We got the lecture about leaving things lying around. Suddenly, his tummy felt better. Still, the fragrance of pumpkin pie upset him for months after Thanksgiving. Precious memories, how they linger!

CHAPTER TWELVE

The Eighties brought about many changes for us all. Mom and Dad dug into Little League baseball and other civic duties in Eastlake. Phil and I raced toward graduation, marriage, and independence, but there were bumps along the way.

I got off the school bus at Taft Elementary School with a stack of papers to share with Mom. Our elementary school offered adult education courses in the evenings, and they were perfect to supplement Mom's lack of formal education. Boy, wrong again!

I raced into our house and showed Mom the enrollment forms. She looked over each with great suspicion before delivering her knockout blow.

"Junior, I know what this is! You're just ashamed of me! You are ashamed of your dumb little mother, right? You can take these papers and stick them where the sun doesn't shine!" Mom growled.

I wanted nothing but help for her 3rd-grade education. Sure, I was tired of her asking me to spell everything, then turning around and calling me "Professor" when irritated. I tried assuring her that the classes were suitable for everyone. Constantly insulted, Mom brooded for hours.

As I prepped for school early the following day, Dad took his coffee and cigarettes from our breakfast nook table. He interrogated me.

"Did you argue with your mother yesterday?" Dad quizzed.

"Yeah, she went over the edge about me suggesting adult learning classes. Then she accused me of being ashamed of her! Man, if she wants to be an ignorant little hillbilly her whole life, then go for it! You cannot help her!' I answered.

A strong streak of light came near our bathroom door that shocked me. I found myself against the back wall, both feet off the floor, and Dad's angry face pressed into mine!

"You ignorant kid! That's your mother you're talking about! My wife, get me? You ever talk like that again, and I'll put you through the wall. If you think you're going to get away with that, pal, then you've got rocks in your head!" Dad fired back.

Dad's elbow crushed my Adam's apple enough for me to taste the bitter juice of my stupidity! With the exchange, I learned that no Round Two is needed. Dad handled any cracks people made about him, but if anyone insulted his wife, The End neared! He stood by his spouse, loved her, and protected her. If anyone attacked her, then it struck him. It couldn't go unanswered.

We began the era known as the "matching t-shirt" span for Mom and Dad. They went to the local Daffy Dan's custom shirt shop and got "I love Emily-I love Gusty" printed on every color in the rainbow. Is Dad a fan? No, but it meant everything to Mom, so he went along. His friends snickered once and then let it drop. There is no depth of love that Dad doesn't display for his bride.

Growing up in his era, Dad saw that poor people wore dungarees or, later, "blue jeans," and he refused to wear them. He believed t-shirts were only "underwear" and should not be a public eyesore. Extreme underdressing happened to Dad in a t-shirt outside our home, but his endurance showed Mom limitless possibilities. That fact remains baffling even after all these years.

Mom went from being part of the Little League concession stand crew to running the operation. Her involvement improved her overall mental health. She also helped produce the annual Little League program book.

The gang pieced together the book using standard typewriters, paper, and glue. Complete team rosters, game schedules, key phone numbers, and sponsor ads were neatly packaged by dedicated souls. While Mom and her crew assembled their part, Dad, ever the salesman, visited local merchants and collected sponsorship support. Countless hours in a labor of love enabled my folks to serve, greet the public, and produce a helpful handbook. It gave them a purpose, and they did it well. Mom appreciated the compliments and loved working alongside Dad in any capacity; their teamwork was evident in their love for each other.

Dad found a gland in his neck that needed removal right away. A stone caused the malfunction, and surgery was scheduled ASAP for St. Vincent Hospital in Cleveland. Dad's confinement yielded a good roommate.

Family and friends paid their respects for a fast release. While Parson and Hettie Mae nearly made things a party, a man named Red *did*! The wild man came along at just the right time.

Dad asked for his electric razor so he could shave. I entered his room, and a strange odor attacked my sensitive nose. Mom said she smelled smoke, too. Dad pointed at the curtain between himself and Red, rolling his eyes and lifting his hands skyward.

Curious, I walked past the curtain and found Mr. Red smoking a large joint, puffing while getting the smoke out of the open window! My face must have said everything.

"Oh, man, you know, I got my own method of healing, dude! This here is all-natural!" Red boasted. I shook my head in disbelief.

Dad said the man's expulsion by the hospital staff seemed imminent. Did he care? Nope.

"Jesus, Emily, that crap is givin' me a terrific headache!" Dad complained. Red said he'd put the "funny" cigarette away in Dad's honor. He asked me to pull the dividing curtain back.

"Hey, you'll, you know I am bi-racial, right? Yeah, a struggle, but now quite cool! See, if I comb my hair forward, then I can look like a white dude in any neighborhood. IF I want to see the brothers, then I comb it back, pick it out, and they see me as one of them! Cool, huh?" Red asked.

We talked and laughed with Red for hours. He got released and wanted our attendance at his birthday party later in the week. We agreed, not knowing what lay ahead.

I worked to cover my automobile addiction and dates, but got stuck at my sub-shop job while my family partied. They promised a visit after, but I didn't bank on it.

Near the end of my evening, Dad brought Mom and Phil in for a snack. Mom stumbled in laughing. Was Mom drunk? Mom is, uh, what?

The greetings were fun, and the hugs were plenty. Mom's bloodshot eyes and mix of barbecue/marijuana scent caught me off guard. Phil leaned over and called it. "Mama be stoned, Gus! Hehehehehe!"

Mom tried ordering one of everything on the menu between belly laughs! A sight to behold!

"Boy, that Red, he is crazy! You know, Junior, he got the best ribs, soul food, and all, but those funny cigarettes he smokes, oh my! He kept these glass tubes a-layin' around. He smokes that, you know, mo-ahna, stuff every time! Hahahaha, your dad stayed away, but I feel a little drunk on it! Hehehehehe!" Mom mustered.

My mother, a woman who hated medications, aspirin, doctors, whatever, stood in front of me, happier than anyone believed! Higher than Cheech and Chong, her motto, "Put that in your pipe and smoke it!" became a reality.

Between laughs, Mom bellowed her infamous sayings. I told her I wished I'd been at the party. Her reply? "Wish in one hand, "spit" in the other, and see which gets filled quicker!" More uproarious laughter followed. She made funny faces, so I stuck my tongue out at her as I filled their order. This response? "No thanks, I use toilet paper!" My co-workers laughed hysterically, congratulating my incredible mom.

Dad confirmed that he helped Mom to the car and that she laughed the entire ride. I couldn't wait for my shift to end! At home, I found Mom sleeping off her indiscretion. Did Red have the miracle cure? We'd never find out, but his method beat shock treatment warnings and antipsychotics.

Dad used his connections to find me a job at Kmart. No grill smell, no late hours, and no drunks at midnight sealed the deal. Kmart employee first class!

Things in the new, clean job were to my liking, except for one assistant manager with the nickname "Dracula" prowling about, seeking souls. Nobody pleased her impossible expectations! Where did I turn?

I complained about "Dracula" one night at dinner. Dad, a strong worker-rights guy, said he hoped for a transfer. Mom took a different approach.

"Junior, you just might win her over! You know, try finding just one thing you like about her and hanging onto that! If the other fellers give her trouble, you don't! Finish your work list and ask for more! She'll figure she can count on you!" Mom advised.

Gee, I hadn't thought of any of that. The woman worked long fourteen-hour days at least once per week. Maybe she'd seen enough grumpy customers and confrontational employees by the time I got there after school. I tried it, and Mom's advice worked 100% within a week! Mom may have been uneducated in the world's eyes, but she was far from dumb. Dad told me that we were to come around for good advice every once in a while. What a revelation.

Dad announced we would see Shirley and Al in Las Vegas during our vacation adventures! AMTRAK rescued us for the two-thousand-mile journey.

We boarded the train in downtown Cleveland at four in the morning. My excitement to see my mentor and confidant, Shirley, kept me from griping. We got luxurious, wide seats to kick back in. A few hours later, Chicago came into view.

The layover at Union Station allowed us to tour the city for a while, eat outstanding hot dogs, and gather snacks for the rest of the ride.

Our train chugged out of the station and into the countryside. America, the beautiful, encompassed us! As Phil and I sought out girls, Mom and Dad settled into their seats. An observation car with a glass ceiling came in handy.

Teens our age ended up together as the day gave way to a night of a million stars across the Western sky. During the hours that passed, we told stories about our homes and schools. Phil and I got bored, and that meant trouble.

Every teen on the train went on a quick scavenger hunt to find "toys" to play with for everyone. We found many things and secured them in our area for further examination. Phil and I grabbed glow sticks near Mom and Dad's seats for train breakdowns. They were the hit of the cache. Nobody found anything more fantastic.

I stood at one end of the observation deck, and Phil waited at the other. We passed the sticks like baseballs over the heads of fellow travelers. We enjoyed a great time until a crewman yelled up to ask what we were doing. We lied, hid the evidence, and settled down for a time to start again later.

One joker decided we should play tag with the funny, bright green sticks. That game morphed into dodgeball and hilarity. Soon, we were winging the bars everywhere until I got nailed with one, and it burst all over my Aerosmith jersey! I cursed over the accident in my favorite shirt. More laughter broke out as others zipped glow sticks at each other. Phil endured one busting on him before the crewman got into our faces!

When we were busted, train personnel marched us to Mom and Dad. With two glowing kids, nobody lied about our involvement. Idiots? Sure. Dad didn't hold back.

"I'm raisin' idiots here, Emily! You take them on a vacation, and this is how you get paid back! You two are something else! Jesus, Mary, and Joseph, what did I do to deserve this? Try using your heads for more than a hat rack!" Dad howled.

Mom agreed and kept her three eyes on us from then on out. (Yes, the third one resides in the back of her head, but it is unverified by physicians.)

Our train broke down in the desert somewhere in Utah. We baked like hams in the July sun in the heat-absorbing train cars with zero electricity! Hours later, we were moving again. The next day provided "Viva Las Vegas!"

Phil and I shared high expectations about *Sin City*. Gee, *everything* appeared legal there. Our folks took us up and down the strip. The sights were sensory overload for us, meaning f-e-m-a-l-e visual stimulation.

Mom and Dad took off many nights to Sam's Town, a quick favorite to frequent. We did the tourist tour of Hoover Dam, Red Rock Canyon, and Lake Mead. The lake disappointed us.

We rolled up to Lake Mead with great excitement. Phil and I took off straight for the water and plowed in. Yuck! It felt like someone ran a hot bath for us before bed. The freaking water wasn't cool! We looked back to see Mom camp herself in the shade, a floppy hat covering her wild hair.

Everyone tried to get Mom to the water and away from the trees. She could not get into the water or away from the cover, so Al spoke up.

"Emily, you gotta get away from those trees! You know, I don't care, but the tarantulas and snakes hide over there." Al said nonchalantly.

Mom levitated, grabbed her belongings, passed roadrunners, and acted like she'd seen Herman Munster at the beach! She must have run the fifty-yard dash in under three seconds!

The rest of the trip satisfied us. The train ride back went well except for another breakdown out West. Dad wrote to AMTRAK about the conditions, and they sent half of our money back for the inconvenience. Another lesson learned.

Dad desired to be close to his siblings scattered from Pennsylvania to Florida. His older brothers and sisters meant the world to him. It was rare for any of the siblings to visit our home. Everyone raised their own families, of course. If we were to be the travelers for Stefanow's sake, so be it. Dad hadn't seen Uncle Tommy for years, so driving to Miami, Florida, in the old wagon took little convincing. Phil loved the idea of sunny beaches and bikinis, so nobody disagreed.

Our old Chevy wagon had seen better days. We needed the space with Mom packing like we were moving on every trip. Seven hours into the journey, we stopped in London, Kentucky, for the mandatory Dog Patch stop and to pick up Mom's brother, Tim. Although an uncle, he felt far more like a brother. Three teens and more fun than a barrel of monkeys set sail for sunny Florida!

Dad cussed with each stop for fuel. The old Chevy loved motor oil as much as gasoline! Despite that, we got into Georgia. Moses took a million sojourners across the desert, while our family had trouble getting five souls to Miami.

Mom's "hungry-sick" stomach acted up an hour later, so Dad pulled into a giant truck stop. Dad rechecked the oil while we piled into the truck stop. We used the facilities and got underway.

The drive through Georgia became long, and three teenage boys got restless. Phil, the biggest joker in the deck, spiced up the ride.

"Hey, Mom, remember when Doctor Simmons wanted to juice you up with those shock treatments? Hahaha! Good times!" Phil retorted.

"Phillip, you shut it back there! I ain't going to listen to your foolishness! That ol' man's crazier than me anyway!" Mom responded.

Phil didn't let it go. Dad, as usual, glared into the back seat through the rearview mirror. Had it been a computer screen, poor ol' Dad's scowl could have etched itself on it.

Phil leaned forward in his seat, reached over the front seat, and applied his hands to Mom's neck. He pretended to make fake bolts and let out a "buzz-buzz" sound to the delight of Tim and me.

"Guys, Mom could have been the next Frankenstein! Hahahaha! Do it, Gus, you know, the Doctor Simmons voice! Come on, man, do it! You've got to!" Phil insisted. I composed myself as Mom flailed her left arm over the seat to smash my kid brother.

"Hello, dare, is Emily dare? This is Doctor Simmons! Muhuhuhahahaha! I want to start your shock treatments, Emily!" I managed to say, in my evil, mad-scientist voice.

Dad's ticked-off face made us laugh ourselves into a head rush! Mom thrashed at us with both arms as the scene got funnier. Once Dad cussed at us for our ignorance, we calmed down for a few miles.

Phil left the men's room last, but no one noticed. He carefully plotted his next move. Out of nowhere, he flipped my ear with a perceived rubber band as I surveyed the peach trees in Georgia.

He then spun around and attacked Tim as well. He kept snapping something unfamiliar as we sat there.

"Phil! Tim yelled, cut it out, you maniac! Sissy, your boy is a-snappin' us back here, and I am going to kill him if he doesn't stop!"

Mom drifted into preoccupation and paid no attention. Then, one snap proved too many, and the foreign object sailed over the front seat and onto the dashboard. Dad ignored the projectile, but Mom did *not* miss it.

"Oh Lord, what in the world? Lord have mercy, who shot this thing up here?" Mom inquired.

Tim and I were not taking the blame for this one! We named Phil the perpetrator in unison.

"Phillip, where did you get this? Oh, Gus, do you see what this is? Phillip, is this from the truck stop floor? You get this near the toilets, you little dummy? You are sick, young man, just sick! I will brain you!" Mom accused.

Dad took a good look and almost wrecked the car. There on the dashboard sat twenty-five cents' worth of birth control. Yes, a condom called the "super-duper" arrived by airborne express!

Tim and I laughed so hard that we cried. Phil didn't muster up a lie nor backtracked his way out of the discovery.

"One quarter, right? I want to see what they look like. Aren't men supposed to carry them? Phil asked.

Mom's furious expression showed itself like the hot summer sun! She couldn't resist asking Dad to pull over so she could teach us a lesson. By now, Dad snickered.

"Emily, they are too big to beat! I want to get to my brother's house! And we both know these guys are growin' up, right? They're boys!"

"Well, they're darn lucky they are so big! I'd still like to pull over and stripe their behinds as my mother did! They'd sing a different tune after that! I am raising jackals, stupid jackals!" Mom squealed with delight.

With no maps and little sense of direction, we got into Miami at two a.m. Dad parked in a shopping center parking lot for shuteye and waited for sunrise.

Three teens in a roomy Chevy wagon tried to sleep. Mom slept for hours. Dad and Phil dozed off, but Tim and I didn't. With our windows cracked open, we hoped to pass out from the heat.

An hour later, Tim said, "Gus, Gus, wake up!"

Dad and I both answered him. "No, he said, Big Gus! There's a feller walkin' around the car and eyeballin' us! I ain't sure, but I bet he ain't up to no good." Tim said in his unmistakable drawl.

Dad sat up higher and surveyed the landscape. Sure enough, a man cased the old Chevy. If only he'd known, Dad might have given it to him since it burned *eighteen* quarts of oil on the trip down!

The stranger shook his head and bumbled away. Three in the morning in Miami meant several more hours before daylight.

Sunrise moved us to a local diner for a hearty breakfast. We noticed Miami cops in the restaurant. Dad trusted them for directions to Uncle Tommy's place.

Both officers quizzed us about accommodations for the previous night. Dad told them our plight and about the visitor we hosted.

"Jesus, one cop said, you better thank your lucky stars, mister! Just last year, families like yours were killed in this very neighborhood. These refugees Castro shipped from his jails are criminals and whack jobs!"

A pale look overtook Dad's face as he threatened me with instant death if I told Mom the truth. We arrived at my uncle's place an hour later with much fanfare.

The visit exceeded our expectations, and the highlight was visiting Uncle Tom's job site, the Orange Bowl stadium!

Phil, Tim, and I arrived, and Uncle Tom told us we owned the place. First, we ran onto the field like maniacs, making fake passes and touchdown runs. It didn't last long.

The chief groundskeeper came from a tunnel, screaming expletives as he ran. Uncle Tom intercepted the man with curses of his own. These were his nephews, he said, and the field belonged to us. Problem solved!

The brief visit ended, and we went back to the Buckeye State. We dropped Tim off in Kentucky, and on the return trip, with just twenty-seven quarts of oil, we arrived home. Dad needed a car intervention, and a new 1983 Chevy Monte Carlo replaced the old oil burner.

Mom and Dad's love for children shone throughout their lives. Not only did they raise their own four kids, but they also tried to bring up many others. Our cousins, friends, nieces, and nephews joined us at home or on trips. Mom said she'd have birthed twenty kids if the Lord saw fit.

Leadership roles for both parents came along as the Eighties closed. Phil and I added grandchildren for Mom and Dad to spoil, but baseball and civic responsibilities kept calling their names, and they answered.

CHAPTER THIRTEEN

The 1990s came at us all with a flourish, meaning the 1980s were busy, but we hadn't seen anything yet!

Dad became the Little League President in the mid-1980s and relished the role. The kids were at the heart of all he did. Under his tutelage, the league excelled and grew. Dad also got involved in fundraising for soccer and football, meaning zero off-season! Privately, city leaders tried talking him into running for mayor. Dad's outspoken views on workers' rights and healthcare were interesting, but he showed zero interest in politics. On top of that, he counted the mayor as one of his closest friends.

Mom excelled as the Ladies' Auxiliary President for Little League. She created teams to work on the concession stand and the annual Program Book. I saw her transformation, which looked nothing short of a miracle. Not a hint of witchcraft talk, spells, or Doctor Simmon's psychotropic medicinal cures came from Mom's lips. Yes, the old superstitions remained, but she'd come out of her shell and broken the grip on whatever held her. Never did she shine more than when serving others.

Parson and Hettie Mae invited our family over for dinner. They had enough food for an army! We felt silly as we sat there while their grown children filled our glasses and set the food on a single dish at a time. We were in a four-star restaurant, getting treated like royalty. *Most* people took advantage of the day and relaxed. Not our Type-A, class AAA father! He said something didn't seem kosher with the picture.

Dad gave Mom a glance that meant he'd speak up whether she liked it or not. She leaned over with her tiny feet pressing on his. Even the familiar "Uh-uh," she'd grunt, did no good.

Dad looked around the room, happy but concerned that we were all together.

"Parson, we've been friends a good long time now, right?" Dad asked.

"Yes, sir, we go way back! Hettie and I just came to Cleveland when we met you. Man, those were good times, but hard times, too." Parson replied.

"Well, as friends, we talk plainly, right?" Dad asked before going on.

"I want us all sitting together, man. Your kids are runnin' around like servants! You and Hettie haven't taken a seat. We ain't no *royalty*! If we're all the same here, then let's all be the same!" Dad insisted.

"Say what? (The famous Parson line, used when Dad lays a load of "bull" on the man!) Yes, we're all equals 'round here. Guess we just weren't thinkin'! Hey, you'll, sit down, everybody!" Parson demanded.

Parson and his entire brood sat beside us. Dad asked him to say grace, warning him how long preachers can talk and how food cools off!

This beautiful scene, in which humans can come together and love one another despite the world's perceived differences, runs counter to American life. If in Christ there's no Jew, no Greek, no enslaved person nor free, no male nor female, did we *live* it in the special moment! Family meant family, plain and simple. Biological or not, race or not, the community comes first and foremost.

Mom and Dad's possessive natures with children reached a pinnacle during these years. Always ready for kids, they raised grandchildren despite busy schedules. For their respective ages, they were seasoned dynamos, as many called them. We still don't know how they did it.

Dad's closest friends nominated him for Eastlake's Citizen of the Year in 1991. Everyone knew he'd hate the publicity if even a shred of the plan got out! Despite the stealthy operation, Mom knew and kept her word while helping the planners. Dad? None the wiser, and that helped.

Dad frequented the mayor's office each week in fundraising mode and asked in advance for guidance on improving festivals and civic pride. He was not one for chit-chat and did not waste the mayor's time.

Mayor Becker beamed whenever Dad visited. He knew the man had a heart of gold and loved his city, so he quickly made time for him.

"Gusty, I feel it's right that I tell you something. I hope you don't mind me letting the cat out of the bag. It's that you've been selected as Eastlake's Citizen of the Year for 1991! Congratulations, friend!" The mayor said.

Poor Dad was flabbergasted and speechless. What an honor! Later in the year, an extensive dinner program followed. Stunned, Dad went home and told Mom, who gave an outstanding performance by acting very surprised. We cheered the well-deserved honor.

One day, while I was visiting, Dad asked if I minded running him around the city for a while. Of course, I did not care, as Dad got warm welcomes everywhere. We visited folks at the city hall, different city departments, and offices.

Dad felt like the "Pope of Eastlake," if I could make the connection. Someone would have created a "Gusty-mobile" if Dad had only asked. We treasured being with him even as adults.

He requested a quick stop by the Little League field for a bathroom break. No good son could deny him that. He got out and went to the men's room, but returned disappointed.

"Jesus Mary, and Joseph, Dad said, I've forgotten my freakin' keys! Now what?"

I pointed at the tree line. Dad's rightful concerns about mosquitoes, possums, skunks, or other rodents attacking him were legitimate. I drove towards the higher grass and told him to fake a look at the car tires. When he did, I got him! Hahaha! The apple doesn't fall far from the tree!

He bent down to take care of business and put a hand on the rear fender. What would any "good" son do? Yep, I let the car inch forward! Let the cussing begin!

Each time he caught up, I just moved another foot or two. What great fun! His threats got louder, though.

"Hey, you're stupid! You know, I gotta get back in sooner or later, sonny-boy!" Dad growled.

One last move forward, a little faster and further got the ol' boy galloping! I chuckled, alone with a tear-streamed face. I let him catch up.

"Jesus, Christopher! You dummy! You tryin' to get me soaked, is that it? Dad yelled.

The more he protested, the more I cried. I tried speaking between belly laughs!

"Oh, now, you'd have done the same to me, so don't expect a pity party over here! What about all the "match-burns-twice" jokes or hot-foot Hell we got? Every scare from the basement you set us up for? Huh?"

A smile broke across Dad's face as he reflected on my reminder, and he knew I spoke the truth! Like a good son, I took him home to change.

Dad stayed a busy soul and ignored his health despite warnings. The cigarette habit he tried to dump after his first heart surgery returned. In 1993, his cardiologist found blockages and insisted on surgery again. I went to St.

Vincent's Hospital again, praying along the way. Our church sent out the prayer chain, too.

The surgery went quickly, and Dad waited in recovery. I stayed a few hours after the nurses let me see him.

Dad lay there in the recovery room, looking around for the next bus out. Open-heart surgery came a long way in eight short years. He seemed surprised that I was there.

I asked how he felt after an abysmal, invasive surgery.

"With my hands, that's how!" was often his golden reply. I rolled my eyes and shook my head.

"How are you set for money? Your Mom has the bankroll in her purse. Get some on your way out. I know they're not givin' away gas yet, huh?" Dad said.

I declined, kissed his forehead, and stopped by Mom's table in the lobby, where she portrayed a bundle of nerves.

"What would I ever do without that stupid, stubborn jackass of a Stefanow man, Junior?" Mom asked me.

I reminded her of his rugged, Greek-Polish, Pennsylvania mountain stock. Fewer worries this time, too. She reminded me that smoking would be the end of him if he did not quit. I agreed, hugged Mom, and left for home. It hung in my mind for days with no answer to her question. What would *any* of us do without Dad? My existence without him was senseless, so I pushed it out of my mind. The thought of my parents' epic board games of "Aggravation" played at the kitchen table made me smile. Each routinely accused the other of cheating. Dad played to knock the opponent backward and laughed like a child each time. Good times indeed!

Mom also kept up with her civic responsibilities. She worked on a citywide bingo program that raised funds for kids' sports programs. She kept the Women's auxiliary humming along and the concession stand stocked at the Little League fields. Mom became Citizen of the Year in 1993. The in-house rivalry brought out the ridiculous, but Mom proved just as worthy as Dad. The city honored the ageless duo.

With every great story of triumph, there will be an occasional "hiccup" that can topple a mountaintop experience. Ours came sooner than expected. It's pure Stefanow-style, if I may say so myself.

The Opening Day of the new Little League fields behind Thomas Jefferson Middle School was humming with excitement. You have perfectly manicured like a professional field, each named for outstanding supporters. Gusty and Emily Stefanow's field emanated a unique ring for thousands of spectators, Ohio Congressional and Senatorial representatives, and the City Council. A news crew filmed it all. Suburban theater displayed itself well.

Before the opening ceremony began, Phil called the concession stand to ask for Mom. Why the importance no one knew. The person on the other end of the line told Phil of Mom's acute busyness. What did he need her for, anyway?

"I'm calling in a *bomb* threat! What do you think, huh?" Phil responded.

Pandemonium began with just one ignorant statement. The concession worker called 9-1-1 and reported the emergency. Within minutes, frightened people took cover near their cars as more police crews arrived. Like everyone else, Mom and Dad hunkered down with the city officials, wondering what lunacy befell them on such an important day.

Hundreds of children and parents awaited an all-clear signal from the Lake County bomb squad. All dugouts and outbuildings were investigated at the concession stand as the crowd waited with bated breath.

Hours dragged by before the signal "all-clear" rang out. A simple false alarm from an idiot called in bomb squads and chaos. Dad and Mom were relieved, confident that the moron would get caught!

A few moments later, the Chief of Police, another of Dad's pals, pulled both parents aside. The mayor leaned in as well, away from prying ears or eyes.

"Gusty and Emily, I don't know how to sugarcoat this thing; I just don't. Here goes: the bomb threat was traced to your house! We have Phil in custody at the station."

Mom and Dad looked at each other blankly, unable to elicit an emotion. "What? Our house? This can't be so! Phillip isn't that dumb!" Dad replied.

The officer restated his sentence more slowly and emphasized that he had Phil in custody. There is a scene from the movie Problem Child where the father says something like, "We're raising Satan!" and then collapses. My folks wanted "damage control," and soon, both faced the music, which was not a fun tune.

Mom stayed with the Little League celebration, unable to get Phil from jail because she'd have beaten his brains in if there were any left in his skull. Dad, the fall guy, went and took Phil home. Arraignment came later. Judgment came when Mom got home that night.

Phil played the victim in his role, and Mom felt like shredding her grown son into human mulch for the city's flower beds! Phil insisted that the person on the phone knew he'd been kidding. This, remember, came in the idyllic world we used to know before September 11th. Phil said, "No harm, no foul," but Mom called him everything but a white man in his living room. She left before she went from Citizen of the Year to Inmate of the Month!

A few days later, the arraignment came, and Dad took Phil by himself again. (Mom didn't calm down for weeks.) Phil faced a judge Dad knew, but the tenseness remained.

The bailiff presented the charges, and the judge looked overwhelmed by the gravity of the idiocy. He read the Ohio statutes that Phil had broken and reminded everyone of the seriousness of the matter. Phil stood motionless, somehow, but fellow suspects began cracking smiles. Phil never held anything in.

"Mister Stefanow, is there something humorous in my courtroom?" The judge asked.

"Well, your honor, it is funny. The idiot at the concession stand should've known better!" Phil replied.

"You created a panic, embarrassed family and friends, and this is all you can say? I cannot believe my ears!" The judge said.

Dad stood beside Phil, unable to believe his ears. He leaned over and whispered to Phil to shut up and take his lumps. The exchange spawned an argument that the judge halted.

"I'll fine you $250 and give you six weeks of community service each weekend in Eastlake. Get out of my courtroom!" the judge said sternly.

Phil and Dad's muffled argument created uproarious laughter in the court, but the judge shut it down.

News of the fiasco spread, and my parents could not avoid the unwanted publicity. Shoulder shrugs accompanied by hugs came from devoted friends and neighbors. At this time in his life, Phil cared little about his community profile. His remorse came later.

Mom and Dad loved the community center, annual fundraisers, dances, and 50/50 raffles. Mom became the impromptu master of ceremonies one year.

Uncomfortable filling in, intimidated by the role, and with Mom, no public speaker, she did her best.

Mom yelled out door prizes from local merchants all evening at the sports fundraiser. A local Egyptian-American named Abood owned a grocery store (Valu-King) and was a great member of Eastlake society. His smile was prominent, his laugh undeniable, and his perpetual good mood lifted spirits everywhere.

A problem arose when Mom announced that a gift certificate from Valu-King Abood had been donated. My folks mispronounced names and never tried correcting themselves. Some took these as an enduring charm, but others did not. Abood fell into the latter category.

Mom took the microphone for Abood's offering after doling out prizes.

"Okay, we got a gift certificate from A-Bob's Valu-King for someone! I'll pull the ticket, you'll. Everybody payin' attention?" Mom asked.

Abood looked disgusted. "Who is this A-Bob?" he said out loud.

Dad heard him and comforted his friend in his own way.

"Hey, A-Bob, maybe you need a drink or somethin', huh? Ain't this a great party? Come on, buddy, let's get a beer!" Dad said.

"Gusty, A-Bob, you speak? I know no A-Bob! My name is Abood, Abood!" Dad's friend exclaimed.

"Why, you're A-Bob, brother! Why do you ask me for your name, buddy? A-Bob, I mean!" Dad answered.

Abood shook his head, muttered something in Arabic, and waltzed away. Dad hunched his shoulders and went on mingling.

In a short break, Mom mingled with her closest friends. They congratulated her on filling in as the MC. As Mom leaned over a table to converse, a city council member rudely smashed her. What happened next, Mom will never forget!

Mom drew back from the blow, and when she did, her false teeth ejected from her open mouth! The launched teeth did a mid-air somersault, whacked the table, and landed in her friend's salad.

Mom, embarrassed, ran around the table, retrieving her choppers at warp speed. She rummaged through the salad, got the teeth, gave them a quick shake, and then stuffed them into her mouth. She ran away and hid for several minutes, unsure how to continue. Dad comforted Mom as best he could.

"Gus, maybe you should finish! I can't face these people!" Mom said.

"Emily, only a few saw what happened! I'm no MC! Just get up there and finish! If anybody says anything, I'll make their teeth fly, okay? Come on now!" Dad assured Mom.

Mom finished the job but paid close attention to her teeth, with the show almost over.

When finished, I stopped to help tear down and clean up, like a good son. The tables had to be broken down and put away, and the floors needed sweeping, and I helped out.

The mayor and several council members milled around, congratulating everyone on a job well done. Mayor Becker asked about life in the Dayton area.

"Things are going well with us, Mayor! Imagine where I'd be today if I hadn't done drugs in high school," I boasted, in jest, of course.

I hadn't realized my parents were behind me. The mayor and council were shocked, looked at each other, and smiled. I grinned, and then everyone broke into good laughter!

Everyone, that is, *except* Mom and Dad. Dad looked disgusted, shook his head, and cussed under his breath. Mom took action on her adult son.

"Stupid, stupid! Said Mom as she pinched my left arm and led me away from the dignitaries. How did I go so wrong with two idiot sons? Did you see those faces? Jesus, Junior, you're as big a dummy as your brother!" Mom insisted.

Too dumb for defense, I chuckled as Mom stood there like Moe Howard, hands on hips, ready to crack me a good one.

Dad couldn't let it rest. He chimed in, too.

"Holy cats, you know, I hoped that one of my kids would make good for himself! Jesus Christopher, between you and Phil, our reputation is down the drain! If this keeps up, we're going to have to move! Holy Toledo, I got two jackasses!" Dad complained.

Sometimes, the emotions that Mom elicited, Dad ignored. Other times, depending on the crisis, they came across as collateral damage alongside his response. The two became one as the First Family of Eastlake, despite their kids appearing to take them down.

My folks always needed the grandchildren around. In a brutal act of bravery, they decided to take six grandchildren to Kings Island amusement park. My kids will never forget it!

Mom and Dad arrived at my place with the usual calamity and mayhem. The six children made enough noise to wake the dead, but nobody cared. It was off to park for the day!

Getting everyone loaded into the van became chore number one. With Mom carrying food and supplies for surviving a nuclear blast, things got tight in the van. With the interior smelling of rank Tabu perfume, stale fart, and Juicy Fruit gum, away they went.

Two adults and one teen against five fidgety kids weren't good odds at the park. Everyone got along fine, even enjoying themselves.

A train ride came up, and Dad wandered away for tickets. Being fifty yards from Mom wasn't enough room for him to ignore her.

"Gus, Gus, *I got...the...money*!" Mom bellowed in front of tens of thousands all around them. Mom was never one to be ignored by anyone.

Dad just looked irritated at his bride. He became the face of the most frustrated married man in America! Sure, he loved his bride to the moon and back, but sometimes he wanted her *sent* there.

"Eh, miserable woman!" Dad muttered as he walked back for the cash. His misery index became the funniest thing on earth, and we never got enough of it.

The ride home was not without fireworks, either. Mom kept Dad awake as the kids were tuckered out and resting—no small chore at night.

"Gus, that windshield is plumb full of bugs! How in the world are you seein' out of that?" Mom yelled.

"Oh, Jesus, Emily, I can see just fine. Leave me alone and sit there quietly for a while! Will you do me that kindness, just for once?" Dad replied.

Mom jabbed some more, and Dad, in a moment of raging anger, put the windshield wipers on with a heavy dose of the fluid. What happened next almost caused World War Three!

As Mom and Dad argued, the windshield got plastered with a greenish-colored liquid that enveloped it! Now, absolute zero visibility reared its head, so much so that Dad obligingly pulled over to the roadside.

Dad opened the hood and, gulping hard, knew he had accidentally put anti-freeze into the windshield washer reservoir! He scrambled up a good lie, only to realize his error.

"Uh, Emily, I need some napkins or something for this windshield. I don't know what happened, but this is a mess. I think maybe one of these radiator hoses is leaking!"

Always skeptical of everything, Mom handed Dad a stack of napkins to wipe off the residue. Her cynical side roared immediately.

"Kids, I think your grandfather did something dumb under that hood before we left. I know it, but I can't *prove* it!" Mom barked.

Poor Dad scraped, cussed, and scraped much harder without much effect. He limped the vehicle to a service station for an actual windshield cleaner. Mom's wrath went on highest alert as he strolled back into the van.

"Gus, I know, I know you done somethin' stupid when you were toppin' off them fluids at the house. Admit it, Big Mister Car Man, you messed it up! Mom yowled.

Dad's anger built up as he drove to find help. He put on his hazard lights and went well under the posted speed limit. He'd not let Mom get by with the lambasting she put on him.

"Jesus, Emily, you try something, right, and this is the thanks you get! I don't know what happened, but I gotta clean the windshield. Got anything productive to say? Miserable woman! Why? Why me, Lord?"

"Stupid, stupid man! I have seen about everything now, especially you not takin' the blame for messin' up!" Mom spouted out.

To add insult to injury, Mom rolled her window and wiped her side glass clean. She pulled the soaked paper towel inside and gave it a good sniff.

"It's anti-freeze, I can smell it! Dumb, dummy tryin' to kill us all!" Mom said forcefully.

Dad drove from the interstate to an open gas station. He parked but never said another word to Mom. He feverishly cleaned every inch of the affected glass, climbed inside, and went on his way. Never again did my folks try such an endeavor on their own. The trip made them realize that slowing down was a reality they faced.

CHAPTER FOURTEEN

Dad's health took a downward turn during his final decade on Earth. His emphysema worsened each year. Annual check-ups were regular except when a shadow showed on an X-ray of his lungs. The doctor assured us not to worry. His diagnosis proved dreadfully wrong.

Mom worried enough for both parents as Dad battled on. With no more heart attacks, he still suffered from low blood pressure and dizziness. Mom often said, "Don't you *die* on me!" Frequent ambulance rides and 9-11 calls punctuated the last chapter of Dad's life. Ever the fighter, he duked it out with both hands against the Angel of Death. Despite the ever-present threat of his failing mortality, he hid his fears well. Scared, he couldn't let it show because of the effect it would have on his bride. Dad talked Mom from the ledge, calmed her many fears, and listened to her in a way no one else had the patience to endure.

Mom kept track of Dad's nitroglycerine pills when he needed them. Doctor Emily stayed abreast of Dad's health, sometimes to his chagrin. Mom herself followed what we dubbed the "Kentucky Health Plan"-that is, see doctors in the emergency room instead of seeing the *undertaker*!

Mom and Dad both dug into their faith. Dad served as an usher at St. Mary Magdalene's Church each week. Mom, despite Baptist/Pentecostal roots, got herself confirmed in Catholicism. Why? She wanted her casket in a church someday, and the Catholics accommodated the request. She joined the Holy Name Society, prayed the rosary with others each week, and visited the sick. The church meant a great deal to them, and they needed the fellowship.

Dad called and asked about biblical tithing. I gave him the usual statistics: just one percent of Catholics will obey, while only two percent of Protestants do. I told him that obedience to God's commands brings unimaginable rewards. We hung up the phone, but not before the customary warning of "Take care of Nikki and the kids!"

A week later, Mom and Dad called again about how giving reflects hearts and wallets. Mom's aggravation mounted on Dad, her "stupid man," for a boo-boo he made at church.

"You see, I went through my wallet and tossed in my usual twenty bucks, but accidentally put in a *hundred-dollar bill!* Mom wanted me to get the change. Even the nuns called and said they'd give change since twenty bucks got marked on the envelope!" Dad explained.

His embarrassment kept him from getting the remaining money. I explained sacrificial giving and that God said, "Test me in this and see if I do not throw open the floodgates of heaven and pour out so much blessing that there will not be room enough to store it," by trusting with our wallets (Malachi 3:10). Nikki and I had seen God move in ways we never envisioned.

Dad thanked me for the "mistake," but Mom disagreed.

Within a week, Dad phoned with glee that I thought he'd won the lottery. His enthusiasm roared through the phone!

"Gusty, you won't believe this! Today I got a letter from the Bureau of Workers' Compensation showing an updated check. Jesus, they're increasing it over five hundred bucks a month! Jeez, I guess that giving stuff is for real, eh?" Dad asked.

I assured him we could not give to receive, but things like this were possible. Sometimes, the "storehouse of blessings" was friendship, good health, or any number of ways that the Lord provides. His faith never wavered after. This teachable moment I relished. Mom came on board, too.

Dad believed every Christian believer should wear "Sunday best" each time in the Lord's house. The man never dressed down for any occasion, wearing jeans and tennis shoes once in his lifetime. He showed reverence through his appearance in church. He stepped over the line just one time.

Being an usher gratified Dad. The interaction with parishioners, priests, and fellow servants highlighted his week. He sensed ownership and authority that matched his personality. A test came that he didn't expect.

A young woman flagged Dad down, complaining that the air conditioning froze her out. She told him, "Set the temperature higher so I'll be more comfortable."

Without missing a beat and with no real malicious intent, Dad replied.

"Well, Miss, *if* you'd put on some clothes, then the air would not bother you so much!" Dad replied, turned around, and walked away.

After the service, the head usher gathered everyone for a short meeting on appropriate conduct.

"Men, our congregation is made up of folks from all over. We serve young, old, and everyone in between. We don't need comments on what anyone wears, okay?"

Dad knew everything directed his way and claimed the infraction. Personal responsibility priorities became his cornerstones.

"Look, if you're talking about the woman in the short, low-cut cocktail dress that must have come from a nightclub, then don't blame these other fellas! I don't regret telling her!" Dad confessed.

Others left, and Dad talked over his judgment about his clothing. Warned not to let it happen again, he took his whole being to restrain it. He grunted and walked away.

The Great Brownout of August 2003 hit Cleveland like a hammer. It could not have come at a worse time, considering my family and Shirley were simultaneously at my parents' place.

The world stopped spinning that day. Even though entire neighborhoods grilled mounds of food to prevent spoilage, the party-like atmosphere continued. Smiling neighbors shared their bounties and cared for one another. What a glimpse of what life on Earth might look like if we loved one another.

Losing power at the hottest time of year could have been better. We spent hours outside until it got too warm, and then we retreated into the cool basement. Dad worked the crowd with ghost stories. I called him out on it because his hogwash wasn't welcome.

"Okay, we gotta ghost called Fred! No lie! We do!" Dad howled.

Group eye-rolling began in earnest but did not last long when a music box on the wall made a complete three-hundred-sixty-degree turn! The box hadn't been touched for years, at least by human hands! The crowd dwindled as a human stampede ascended the stairs, rivaling anything on the Serengeti Plain! Dad's matter-of-fact demeanor took over.

"I told you the joint *is* haunted. Oh, he doesn't bother anybody. Maybe misplaces some things, that's it!"

The "frozen-chosen" of us looked around in disbelief. I'd heard attic noises for decades, and Dad passed them off as raccoons or squirrels on the roof. My reply? "Why do they wear what sounds like work boots, huh?" I never got an answer.

Even after Robin Welch revealed that séances were held in the *basement* years before we moved in, Mom hinted at something otherworldly. Mom being well-healed from the breakdowns meant that I couldn't press her back toward the dark side. No way!

Haunted or not, Alva Drive became the homestead we'd always been proud to own. Through hundreds of parties, we entertained the masses. Rarely did silence last long. Mom and Dad couldn't have taken it anyway.

Dad's surprise 75th birthday event had us at Linda's, but we parked our cars with neighbors nearby, so we did not raise suspicions. Dad's heart was touched; the man with everything had misty eyes over the occasion.

Weeks later, Dad's lung doctor saw something odd on an X-ray. He ordered a lung biopsy, and Dad waffled back and forth on getting one. When an army of us showed up at the Cleveland Clinic-Lake West hospital in May 2004, we convinced Dad that doctors needed a look.

Hours passed as the group waited in the vast seating area. Nobody wanted to think the unthinkable. Prayers went up across the country for Dad. Mom chewed gum, walked the hallways, or talked about how the grandkids were growing.

The cancer doctor performing the procedure gave us the verdict. Dad's lung cancer showed in multiple areas, and aggressive chemotherapy became the answer. A rush of tears, moans, and gasps came over the crowd. Who wants such news?

Dad's lung doctors deflated for the clear view of its invasive monster. He stayed a week in the hospital as we struggled with our new reality. Mom couldn't comprehend what had gone on. Losing Dad meant that there'd be *no* life without him. We didn't know we'd lose Dad in less than ninety days.

So began the treatment days and doctor visits. When Dad got the diagnosis after the biopsy, he became philosophical about it. His thought turned into disgust and alarm.

"Jesus, Mary, and Joseph! My mother-in-law always said she'd outlive me, and doggone it, she is right! She said, "I'll outlive you, you forner!" She called it! Oh, that old bag!" Dad complained. His gift for making the mundane and severe downright comical endeared him to everyone.

"I guess I should never have said, 'Jaybird, if only the good die young, then you will live *forever*!' I ended up cursing myself. Miserable old woman!" Dad remarked.

Mom and Dad lived closer than I'd ever seen them. Always affectionate, they ramped up the little kisses, hugged longer, and gazed into each other's eyes like newlyweds. Time became short, and neither voiced it. Their love story was complicated, but its ups and downs were normal. Five decades together were not by accident or chance. Their marital bliss seemed as unique as their DNA.

Dad became introspective and studious about life's meaning. He related stories he had never heard before. Dad's whole existence revolved around his Stefanow family and its disintegration. His earnest attempts to unite the Stefanow clan seemed like failures, but he believed *someone* had to try. Trying would do one thing: Honor Mom and Pop Stefanow long after passing. He wasn't sure how he'd fared, and that bothered him.

Dad grieved his parents and their love. He wanted his legacy like theirs. From the bed-tucking at night, "bear hugs," his spirit provided love, acceptance, and grace. He feared no collaboration or compromise that yielded unity. He didn't care who got credit for mission accomplishment. He wanted unity for humanity. He valued peace more than most.

We routinely played *"Do you remember when..."* to pass the time. Dad got himself so tickled, regaling us with stories of his childhood! He went down a hill on a little red wagon at super speed. Uncle Tom lassoed him around the neck and almost broke it! Mom Stefanow nearly suffered a breakdown! Dad broke his leg running down a coal pile and came home in a wheelbarrow! Dad ran through pine trees. One branch scratched his face wide open. Mom Stefanow gave him cash to see the doctor. What did he do? He shot pool instead. Infection set in, and a priest came in for Last Rites. An airplane brought in a new drug called Penicillin, which saved him! He climbed towers at a football field one hundred feet high. Once on top, he and his brothers rocked them back and forth!

I took Mom and Dad to Our Lady of Lourdes Shrine in Euclid. As Dad prayed, Mom wept, and I did my best to stay strong. I read John chapter 14, where Jesus explains His Father's house has many mansions. We drew a crowd while I read the Scriptures. Some teared up while others silently listened. Not one soul went untouched that day.

Mom and Dad did more handholding than usual. With more cuddles on the couch, they were careful with the oxygen cables. Dad shrieked, "Wouldn't that be a heck of a way to go? Strangled by your own cables? Sheesh!" Laughter happened until the end for him. Dad dozed off one afternoon. He slept as Mom made small talk, and neither talked over the apparent elephant in the room. Instead, we danced around the topic and marveled over Dad's toughness.

Dad woke up with a snap of his neck. His eyes popped open, and he smiled. "Wow, he said, I walked in a garden with the Lord, and there were the most beautiful flowers you can imagine! Emily, heaven is next when I leave here!"

Mom asked Dad to find a bench when he gets there while he waits for her. He said he'd be there in his best Sunday clothes. He knew the clock ticked for him on that time card in the sky.

Cleveland Clinic's world-famous cancer doctor gave Dad two chemo treatments and then suspended them. Dad couldn't endure the toll it took on his weakened body. Hospice came into view as the sight no one wanted to see.

The beautiful lakeside Hospice facility comforted everyone except Mom! She shopped and occupied her mind, using the defense mechanism she had developed over the years. When several patients passed, Mom exclaimed, "They are dropping like flies in this place!" Phil and I laughed silly as Dad disapproved, but then smiled, too. Dad tells Mom he'll die at home if it's easier, and this is the depth of his deep love for his bride. His love knew no bounds with his beautiful woman from Kentucky. He felt that she needed no hurt beyond the current problems. I found no fault in that.

Many times, the last few months, Dad leaned over and said, "Emily, I have *always* loved you. Always." Mom replied the same way, then added, "I love you, you crazy forner!" They'd kiss and go on about their business. Dad's passing would *not* stop the love they'd developed over the decades. Dad's "very happy guy" mentality stemmed from having his beautiful Emily and his kids. No matter what life threw at him, Dad took it in stride.

My conversations were with Dad while Mom anesthetized herself with her shopping addiction. Dad preferred she do anything other than sit and stare at him as his final days wound down. Everyone handled the crisis their way.

I asked Dad what bothered him. He says a *thirteen*-year-old boy has cancer, again, and is terminal too. He will never have a date, a wife, kids, or anything. Dad is 75 and smoked himself to death after dodging the Grim Reaper many times! "Feel sorry for the young fella, not me!" His empathy is legendary to everyone.

Did Dad harbor regrets about his life? Sure, he wished he had behaved better in his youth. The *pain* he put into Mom Stefanow's eyes with delinquency, reform school, and general mayhem haunted him. Pop Stefanow's anger came from seeing his wife suffer at his son's hands. Of the Stefanow children, Dad felt most ornery. By all accounts, he held the crown by a wide margin.

Dad felt he might have been a better husband and Father, even though his children thought he deserved sainthood for his endurance. He recalled an instance long forgotten.

Women folk derisively called a neighbor "Bikini" for her skimpy (by 1970s standards) swimwear choices. She reportedly ran outside just before the mailman made his daily rounds.

On a warm summer day, Dad caught a fleeting, sideways glance of "Bikini," the kind only married men eventually perfect, and Mom *busted* him! Uh oh!

"Gus, you want to put those eyes back in your darn head? I saw that! Jesus, you and *my* Father can't help crickin' them necks when she's out showin' off what the Good Lord gave her! You two want to see her *nude*? Okay, it sure wouldn't take much strippin' that string off she's a-wearin'!" Mom roared.

"Holy Toledo, Emily! You act like a man ain't got two good eyes! Being married doesn't make a man blind! Jesus, I bet Ray Charles saw that!" Dad replied.

I collapsed on the hospital bed beside Dad in a fit. He always made us laugh even more than he would've liked.

What riled Dad about his offspring? Dad said the lack of *respect* for Mom made him angry. He named Phil and me the most disrespectful, hands down. He told us that our mouths never let up, cracking jokes and making fun of everyone. My one defense I put out there.

"Holy mackerel, Dad, she says stupid things! How do we ignore that?" I asked, knowing better but asking for posterity. His reply?

"Let her talk, let her talk! That's what I always tried. You gotta let your mother have her *say*!"

Dad's daughters were not without fault. How did they get arrogant from their upbringing? They clashed more with Mom than we boys did. Dad wanted it documented that the sacrifices made by *both* folks ushered all his kids into adulthood! He said we should never forget that fact.

Dad knew his kids loved *him* dearly, but he wanted that love to extend to Mom, too. He knew she'd need it to hang on without him. Over time, his offspring realized that *nobody* loved Mom as he did. No substitute for Dad's leadership and care would ever come this way again.

I asked for advice for a long, happy matrimony. Dad said two people "gotta work together or it won't last. Apologize quickly and mean it! Never forget *your* faults when looking at your spouse!" Dad unloaded a little.

"You kids know I'm no saint, and neither is Mom! How many times did I get down on my knees and ask God to let me keep my beautiful Emily! What a fool! Yes, the gamblin', drinkin', and the stupid things I did or said didn't help! We never went to bed mad at each other!"

Other caveats concerned our beliefs. Dad wanted a Christian heritage passed along.

"Get and keep your kids in church as long as they'll go! I told you there ain't, but one God, but people worship Him differently. Muslims do their thing, Jews another. Christians are divided into a million pieces. One God, one Lord Jesus- be like Him. You know, the only thing wrong with the world is *people*!"

Father Ted came by on my last day with Dad and proclaimed that Dad would be around a while longer. Dad and I watched the Mayberry Band annihilate patriotic music, and he smiled. The haunting, hollow look in his eyes didn't comfort me. I kissed his forehead, squeezed him, and insisted I'd see him later. He recalled Papaw's last few breaths and reminded me never to watch anyone die, so I honored his command and avoided his final hours. The reality set in on the ride home, and I felt helpless. I thanked God for the forty years with Dad, but truth be known, I wanted forty more.

I went to work in an attempt at normalcy. Nikki showed up at the Dayton VA one afternoon; it was the only time I didn't want to see her. She shook her head and said Dad's *gone*. It felt like a portion of the night sky went out, *never to be lit again*. The most formidable, strongest man on Earth proved mortal. I felt less safe, less loved, less protected, and my world much darker than before. I became the family "point man" while ill-prepared and woefully ignorant.

Mom's shock and irreconcilable tears met us when we arrived in Eastlake. I lay on Dad's hospital bed, and it comforted me. We all mourned in the saddest gathering on Earth. We finalized funeral arrangements as we fumbled through life for a few days, simply existing.

Mom asked that I speak before more than three hundred people at the funeral, and I didn't refuse. I got through it by the grace of God and many prayers.

Parson and Dad's friend Johnny Sizemore dressed in style to remember the man. Both credited Dad with giving them a career and lifestyle they wouldn't have had otherwise. They loved Dad as their own.

"You know, your daddy couldn't quote chapter and verse like some, but man, he lived the gospel! He showed folks the love of God, even the undeserving! Oh Lord, I loved this man so much!" Parson said with tears in his eyes. Tributes were common and priceless.

A one-hundred-car procession went to All Souls Cemetery in Kirtland. The priest blessed the body in the mausoleum dome, and the crowd filtered out. I kissed the blue casket and promised to see my hero in the afterlife. I don't know how I stood that day except for the divine intervention.

Mom lived deliriously with grief for years after Dad's passing. Her gangly, olive-skinned "forner" boy, her best Christmas present *ever*, left her. What kept her going? Her faith, family, and perhaps the words of *their* song, "Maybe you'll be there"-1947:

> *"You said your arms would always hold me*
> *You said your lips were mine alone to kiss*
> *Now, after all those things you told me*
> *How can it end like this?*
> *And then your arms will always hold me*
> *Your lips will be mine alone to kiss*
> *I'll never have to hurry to the door*
> *Cause, baby, you'll be there*
> *Baby, you'll be there*
>
> *Maybe you'll be there."*

The family reunion is coming when we gather on the other side. What a party that will be!

The End

Also by GUS STEFANOW

She called me TETCHED
Spite Work
A Match Struck in Akron
Shooby is the Word
Hybrid Hillbilly
Repartee
Seconds From Eternity

Watch for more at https://www.facebook.com/
profile.php?id=100089276174602.

About the Author

Author Gus Stefanow resides in beautiful Ohio. Semi-retired, he keeps busy with grandchildren and supporting his wife's non-profit organization. He writes to inspire using humor, love, and a healthy dose of irreverence. His simple theology is to love God-love people.

Spite Work, published in 2022, chronicles the author's faith journey. A Match Struck in Akron, released in 2023, is a tribute to his parents' fifty years of love and combat, sometimes called marriage.

Read more at https://www.facebook.com/profile.php?id=100089276174602.